Dissent

from the

Majority Report

of the

Financial Crisis
Inquiry Commission

⤶

Peter J. Wallison

January 2011
American Enterprise Institute for Public Policy Research
pwallison@aei.org

Distributed by arrangement with the Rowman & Littlefield Publishing Group, 4501 Forbes Boulevard, Suite 200, Lanham, Maryland 20706. To order, call toll free 1-800-462-6420 or 1-717-794-3800. For all other inquiries, please contact AEI Press, 1150 Seventeenth Street, N.W., Washington, D.C. 20036, or call 1-800-862-5801.

Library of Congress Cataloging-in-Publication Data

Wallison, Peter J.
    Dissent from the majority report of the Financial Crisis Inquiry Commission / Peter J. Wallison.
        p.   cm.
    Includes bibliographical references.
    ISBN-13: 978-0-8447-7230-1 (pbk.)
    ISBN-10: 0-8447-7230-5 (pbk.)
    ISBN-13: 978-0-8447-7231-8 (ebook)
    ISBN-10: 0-8447-7231-3 (ebook)
1. Global Financial Crisis, 2008-2009. 2. United States. Financial Crisis Inquiry Commission. I. Title.
    HB3722.W345 2011
    330.973'0931—dc22

Printed in the United States of America

Contents

List of Illustrations

Preface

On February 16, 2011, the Financial Services Committee of the U.S. House of Representatives held a hearing on the Financial Crisis Inquiry Commission. As one of four members of the Commission who appeared as witnesses, I was given five minutes to summarize my written testimony (available at http://www.aei.org/speech/100193) and was asked to comment on the implications of my dissent for the Dodd-Frank Act. The following is my oral statement.

Chairman Bachus, ranking member Frank and members of the Committee:

By June of 2008, there were 27 million subprime and Alt-A mortgages in the U.S. financial system—half of all mortgages. These weak and risky loans had begun to default in unprecedented numbers when the 1997–2007 bubble began to deflate, and by 2008 many financial institutions that held these mortgages—or mortgage-backed securities based on them—were in trouble.

No one doubts that it was the failure of these mortgages—what was known at the time as the mortgage meltdown—that caused the financial crisis. Nothing like this had ever happened before. In previous bubbles, the number of subprime loans was very small, and losses when they deflated were generally confined to local areas. In this bubble, the mortgage losses were large and the losses international.

In light of these facts, the question the Commission should have answered—and did not—was why there were so many bad mortgages outstanding in 2008? Obviously, there had been a serious decline in underwriting standards—something else that had never happened before.

Neither the Commission nor the other dissenters ever advanced a plausible explanation for the decline in underwriting standards. Both seemed to assume that easy credit automatically produces subprime loans. But this is far from obvious.

Before the 2008 crisis, the United States had frequently experienced periods of low interest rates, large flows of funds from abroad, and housing bubbles. We also had the same regulatory structure and relied on financial institution managements to anticipate risks. None of these conditions or factors—separately or together—had ever before resulted in a mortgage-based international financial crisis.

Under these circumstances, it is logical to focus on the one unprecedented element in the U.S financial system before the crisis—the large number of subprime and other risky loans. My dissent focuses on the only plausible explanation for the build-up of these loans—U.S. government housing policy.

Beginning in 1992, with the imposition of affordable housing requirements on the GSEs, mortgage underwriting standards began to erode. HUD caused this erosion by raising the affordable housing goals through the Clinton and Bush administrations, until more than half of all loans the GSEs had to buy were required to be made to borrowers at or below the median income where they lived.

In addition, the GSEs were put into competition with FHA, insured banks under the Community Reinvestment Act, and subprime lenders—all of whom were looking for borrowers who were also at or below the median income. Prime loans were difficult to find among these borrowers. So, to acquire the loans the government was demanding, underwriting standards had to be reduced. By 2000, for example, Fannie was offering to buy mortgages with no downpayment.

My dissent details how these weak government-mandated loans caused the growth of the bubble; how the bubble created the private label market for securities backed by subprime loans; and how the failure of all these weak loans destroyed the value of the mortgage backed securities and thus weakened financial institutions around the world.

Finally, the Commission majority's report propagates the false idea that the GSEs bought these risky loans not because of the affordable housing requirements but to regain market share or for profit. My dissent documents that this is not true. For example, this quote from Fannie's 2006 10-K report:

[W]e have made, and continue to make, significant adjustments to our mortgage loan sourcing and purchase strategies in an effort to meet HUD's increased housing goals and new subgoals. These strategies include entering into some purchase and securitization transactions with lower expected economic returns than our typical transactions. We have also relaxed some of our underwriting criteria to obtain goals-qualifying mortgage loans and increased our investments in higher-risk mortgage loan products that are more likely to serve the borrowers targeted by HUD's goals and subgoals, which could increase our credit losses.

Could it be any clearer? The deterioration in underwriting standards was caused by U.S. government policy, and this caused the financial crisis—not a lack of regulation or a failure of risk management.

In my view, then, the Dodd-Frank Act was not soundly based and will not prevent a future financial crisis unless U.S. housing policies are changed.

INTRODUCTION

Why a Dissent?

The question I have been most frequently asked about the Financial Crisis Inquiry Commission (the "FCIC" or the "Commission") is why Congress bothered to authorize it at all. Without waiting for the Commission's insights into the causes of the financial crisis, Congress passed and President Obama signed the Dodd-Frank Act (DFA), far-reaching and highly consequential regulatory legislation. Congress and the President acted without seeking to understand the true causes of the wrenching events of 2008, perhaps following the precept of the President's chief of staff: "Never let a good crisis go to waste." Although the FCIC's work was not the full investigation to which the American people were entitled, it has served a useful purpose by focusing attention again on the financial crisis and whether—with some distance from it—we can draw a more accurate assessment than the media did with what is often called the "first draft of history."

To avoid the next financial crisis, we must understand what caused the one from which we are now slowly emerging, and take action to avoid the same mistakes in the future. If there is doubt that these lessons are important, consider the ongoing efforts to amend the Community Reinvestment Act of 1977 (CRA). Late in the last session of the 111th Congress, a group of Democratic Congress members introduced H.R. 6334. This bill, which was lauded by House Financial Services Committee Chairman Barney Frank as his "top priority" in the lame duck session of that Congress, would have extended the CRA to all "U.S. nonbank financial companies," and thus would apply to even more of the national economy the same government social policy mandates responsible for the mortgage meltdown and the financial crisis. Fortunately, the bill was not acted upon. Because of the recent election, it is unlikely that supporters of H.R. 6334 will have the power to adopt similar legislation in the next Congress, but in the future, other

lawmakers with views similar to Barney Frank's may seek to mandate similar requirements. At that time, the only real bulwark against the government's use of private entities
for social policy purposes will be a full understanding of how these policies were connected to the financial crisis of 2008.

Like Congress and the Obama administration, the Commission's majority erred in
assuming that it knew the causes of the financial crisis. Instead of pursuing a thorough
study, the Commission's majority used its extensive statutory investigative authority to
seek only the facts that supported its initial assumptions—that the crisis was caused by
"deregulation" or lax regulation, greed and recklessness on Wall Street, predatory lending in the mortgage market, unregulated derivatives, and a financial system addicted to
excessive risk taking. The Commission did not seriously investigate any other cause and
did not effectively connect the factors it investigated to the financial crisis. The majority's
report covers in detail many elements of the economy before the financial crisis that the
authors did not like, but generally fails to show how practices that had gone on for many
years suddenly caused a worldwide financial crisis. In the end, the majority's report turned
out to be a just-so story *about* the financial crisis, rather than a report on what *caused* the
financial crisis.

What Caused the Financial Crisis?

George Santayana is often quoted for the aphorism that "those who cannot remember the
past are condemned to repeat it." Looking back on the financial crisis, we can see why
the study of history is so often contentious and why revisionist histories are so easy to
construct. There are always many factors that could have caused an historical event; the
difficult task is to discern which, among a welter of possible causes, were the significant
ones—the ones without which history would have been different. Using this standard, I
believe that the *sine qua non* of the financial crisis was U.S. government housing policy,
which led to the creation of 27 million subprime and other risky loans—half of all mortgages in the United States—which were ready to default as soon as the massive 1997–2007
housing bubble began to deflate. If the U.S. government had not chosen this policy path—
fostering the growth of a bubble of unprecedented size and an equally unprecedented
number of weak and high-risk residential mortgages—the great financial crisis of 2008
would never have occurred.

Initiated by Congress in 1992 and pressed by the U.S. Department of Housing and
Urban Development (HUD) in both the Clinton and George W. Bush administrations, the
U.S. government's housing policy sought to increase home ownership in the United States
through an intensive effort to reduce mortgage underwriting standards. In pursuit of this
policy, HUD used (i) the affordable housing requirements imposed by Congress in 1992 on
the government-sponsored enterprises (GSEs) Fannie Mae and Freddie Mac, (ii) its control
over the policies of the Federal Housing Administration (FHA), and (iii) a "Best Practices
Initiative" for subprime lenders and mortgage banks to encourage greater subprime and
other high-risk lending. HUD's key role in the growth of subprime and other high-risk
mortgage lending is covered in detail in Part III.

Ultimately, all these entities, as well as insured banks covered by the CRA, were compelled to compete for mortgage borrowers who were at or below the median income in the areas in which they lived. This competition caused underwriting standards to decline, increased the numbers of weak and high-risk loans far beyond what the market would produce without government influence, and contributed importantly to the growth of the 1997–2007 housing bubble.

When the bubble began to deflate in mid-2007, the low-quality and high-risk loans engendered by government policies failed in unprecedented numbers. The effect of these defaults was exacerbated by the fact that few, if any, investors—including housing market analysts—understood at the time that Fannie Mae and Freddie Mac had been acquiring large numbers of subprime and other high-risk loans in order to meet HUD's affordable housing goals.

Alarmed by the unexpected delinquencies and defaults that began to appear in mid-2007, investors fled the multi-trillion-dollar market for mortgage-backed securities (MBS), dropping MBS values—especially those MBS backed by subprime and other risky loans—to fractions of their former prices. Mark-to-market accounting then required financial institutions to write down the value of their assets—reducing their capital positions and causing great investor and creditor unease. The mechanism by which the defaults and delinquencies on subprime and other high-risk mortgages were transmitted to the financial system as a whole is covered in detail in Part II.

In this environment, the government's rescue of Bear Stearns in March of 2008 temporarily calmed investor fears but created a significant moral hazard; investors and other market participants reasonably believed after the rescue of Bear that all large financial institutions would also be rescued if they encountered financial difficulties. However, when Lehman Brothers—an investment bank even larger than Bear—was allowed to fail, market participants were shocked; suddenly, they were forced to consider the financial health of their counterparties, many of which appeared weakened by losses and the capital write-downs required by mark-to-market accounting. This caused a halt to lending and a hoarding of cash—a virtually unprecedented period of market paralysis and panic that we know as the financial crisis of 2008.

Weren't There Other Causes of the Financial Crisis?

Many other causes of the financial crisis have been cited, including some in the report of the Commission's majority, but for the reasons outlined below, none of them alone—nor all in combination—provides a plausible explanation of the crisis.

Low Interest Rates and a Flow of Funds from Abroad. Claims that various policies or phenomena—such as low interest rates in the early 2000s or financial flows from abroad—were responsible for the growth of the housing bubble, do not adequately explain either the bubble or the destruction that occurred when the bubble deflated. The United States has had housing bubbles in the past—most recently in the late 1970s and late 1980s—but when these bubbles deflated, they did not cause a financial crisis. Similarly, other developed countries experienced housing bubbles in the 2000s, some even larger than the U.S. bubble, but when their bubbles deflated the housing losses were small. Only in the United States did the deflation of the most recent housing bubble cause a financial meltdown and a serious financial crisis. The reason for this is that only in the United States did subprime and other risky loans constitute half of all outstanding mortgages when the bubble deflated. It wasn't the size of the bubble that was the key; it was its content. The 1997–2007 U.S. housing bubble was in a class by itself. Nevertheless, demand by investors for the high yields offered by subprime loans stimulated the growth of a market for securities backed by these loans. This was an important element in the financial crisis, although the number of mortgages in this market was considerably smaller than the number fostered directly by government policy. Without the huge number of defaults that arose out of U.S. housing policy, defaults among the mortgages in the private market would not have caused a financial crisis.

Deregulation or Lax Regulation. Explanations that rely on lack of regulation or deregulation as a cause of the financial crisis are also deficient. First, no significant deregulation of financial institutions occurred in the last thirty years. The repeal of a portion of the Glass-Steagall Act, frequently cited as an example of deregulation, had no role in the financial crisis.[1] The repeal was accomplished through the Gramm-Leach-Bliley Act of 1999, which allowed banks to affiliate for the first time since the New Deal with firms engaged in underwriting or dealing in securities. There is no evidence, however, that any bank got into trouble because of a securities affiliate. The banks that suffered losses because they held low-quality mortgages or MBS were engaged in activities—mortgage lending—always permitted by Glass-Steagall; the investment banks that got into trouble (Bear Stearns, Lehman and Merrill Lynch) were not affiliated with large banks, although they had small bank affiliates that do not appear to have played any role in mortgage lending or securities trading. Moreover, the Federal Deposit Insurance Corporation Improvement Act of 1991 (FDICIA) substantially increased the regulation of banks and savings and loan institutions (S&Ls) after the S&L debacle in the late 1980s and early 1990s, and it is noteworthy that FDICIA—the most stringent bank regulation since the adoption of deposit insurance—failed to prevent the financial crisis.

The Shadow Banking Business. The large investment banks—Bear, Lehman, Merrill, Goldman Sachs, and Morgan Stanley—all encountered difficulty in the financial crisis, and the Commission majority's report lays much of the blame for this at the door of the Securities and Exchange Commission (SEC) for failing to adequately supervise them. It is true that the SEC's supervisory process was weak, but many banks and S&Ls—stringently regulated under FDICIA—also failed. This casts doubt on the claim that if investment banks had been regulated like commercial banks—or had been able to offer insured deposits like commercial banks—then they would not have encountered financial difficulties. The reality is that the business model of the investment banks was quite different from banking; it was to finance a short-term trading business with short-term liabilities such as repurchase

---

1. See, e.g., Peter J. Wallison, "Deregulation and the Financial Crisis: Another Urban Myth," *Financial Services Outlook*, American Enterprise Institute, October 2009.

agreements (often called "repos"). This made them especially vulnerable in the panic that occurred in 2008, but it is not evidence that the existence of investment banks, or the quality of their regulation, was a *cause* of the financial crisis.

Failures of Risk Management. Claims that there was a general failure of risk management in financial institutions or excessive leverage or risk taking are part of what might be called a "hindsight narrative." With hindsight, it is easy to condemn managers for failing to see the dangers of the housing bubble or the underpricing of risk that now looks so clear. However, the FCIC interviewed hundreds of financial experts, including senior officials of major banks, bank regulators, and investors. It is not clear that any of them—including the redoubtable Warren Buffett—was sufficiently confident about an impending crisis to put real money behind his or her judgment. Human beings have a tendency to believe that things will continue to go in the direction they are going, and are good at explaining why this must be so. Blaming the crisis on the failure to foresee it is facile and of little value for policymakers, who cannot legislate prescience. The fact that virtually all participants in the financial system failed to foresee this crisis—as they failed to foresee every other crisis—does not tell us anything about why this crisis occurred or what we should do to prevent the next one.

Securitization and Structured Products. Securitization—often pejoratively described as the "originate to distribute process"—has also been blamed for the financial crisis. But securitization is only a means of financing. If securitization was a cause of the financial crisis, so was lending. Are we then to blame lending? For decades, without serious incident, securitization has been used to finance car loans, credit card loans and jumbo mortgages that were not eligible for acquisition by Fannie Mae and Freddie Mac. The problem was not securitization itself, it was the weak and high-risk loans that were securitized. Under the category of securitization, it is necessary to mention the role of collateralized debt obligations, known as CDOs. These instruments were "toxic assets" because they were ultimately backed by the subprime mortgages that began to default in huge numbers when the bubble deflated, and it was difficult to determine where those losses would ultimately settle. CDOs, accordingly, for all their dramatic content, were just another example of the way in which subprime and other high-risk loans were distributed throughout the world's financial system. The question is still why so many weak loans were created, not why a system that securitized good assets could also securitize bad ones.

Credit Default Swaps and Other Derivatives. Despite a diligent search, the FCIC never uncovered evidence that unregulated derivatives, particularly credit default swaps (CDS), were a significant contributor to the financial crisis through "interconnections." The only company known to have failed because of its CDS obligations was AIG (American International Group), and that firm appears to have been an outlier. Blaming CDS for the financial crisis because one company did not manage its risks properly is like blaming lending generally when a bank fails. Like everything else, derivatives can be misused, but there is no evidence that the "interconnections" among financial institutions alleged to have caused the crisis were significantly enhanced by CDS or derivatives generally. For example, Lehman Brothers was a major player in the derivatives market, but the Commission found no indication that Lehman's failure to meet its CDS and other derivatives obligations caused significant losses to any other firm, including those that had written CDS on Lehman itself.

Predatory Lending. The Commission's report also blames predatory lending for the large buildup of subprime and other high-risk mortgages in the financial system. This might be a plausible explanation if there were evidence that predatory lending was so widespread as to have produced the volume of high-risk loans that were actually originated. In predatory lending, unscrupulous lenders take advantage of unwitting borrowers. This undoubtedly occurred, but it also appears that many people who received high-risk loans were predatory borrowers, or engaged in mortgage fraud, because they took advantage of low mortgage underwriting standards to benefit from mortgages they knew they could not pay unless rising housing prices enabled them to sell or refinance. The Commission was never able to shed any light on the extent to which predatory lending occurred. Substantial portions of the Commission majority's report describe abusive activities by some lenders and mortgage brokers, but do not give any indication of how many such loans were originated. Further, the majority's report fails to acknowledge that most of the buyers for subprime loans were government agencies or private companies complying with government affordable housing requirements.

Why Couldn't We Reach Agreement?

After the majority's report is published, many people will lament that it was not possible to achieve a bipartisan agreement on the facts. It may be a surprise that I am asking the same question. If the Commission's investigation had been an objective and thorough investigation, many of the points I raise in this dissent would have been known to the other Commissioners before reading this dissent, and perhaps would have been influential with them. Similarly, I might have found facts that changed my own view. But the Commission's investigation was not structured or carried out in a way that could ever have garnered my support or, I believe, the support of the other Republican members.

One glaring example will illustrate the Commission's lack of objectivity. In March 2010, Edward Pinto, a resident fellow at the American Enterprise Institute (AEI) who had served as chief credit officer at Fannie Mae, provided to the Commission staff a seventy-page, fully sourced memorandum on the number of subprime and other high-risk mortgages in the financial system immediately before the financial crisis. In that memorandum, Pinto recorded that he had found over 25 million such mortgages (his later work showed that there were approximately 27 million).[2] Since there are about 55 million mortgages in the United States, Pinto's research indicated that, as the financial crisis began, *half* of all U.S. mortgages were of inferior quality and liable to default when housing prices were no longer

---

2. Edward Pinto, "Triggers of the Financial Crisis" (Triggers memo), http://www.aei.org/paper/100174.

rising. In August, Pinto supplemented his initial research with a paper documenting the efforts of HUD, over two decades and through two administrations, to increase home ownership by reducing mortgage underwriting standards.[3]

This research raised important questions about the role of government housing policy in promoting the high-risk mortgages that played such a key role in both the mortgage meltdown and the financial panic that followed. Any objective investigation of the causes of the financial crisis would have looked carefully at this research, exposed it to the members of the Commission, taken Pinto's testimony, and tested the accuracy of Pinto's research. But the Commission took none of these steps. Pinto's research was never made available to the other members of the FCIC, or even to the Commissioners who were members of the subcommittee charged with considering the role of housing policy in the financial crisis.

Accordingly, the Commission majority's report ignores hypotheses about the causes of the financial crisis that any objective investigation would have considered, while focusing solely on theories that have political currency but far less plausibility. This is not the way a serious and objective inquiry should have been carried out, but that is how the Commission used its resources and its mandate.

There were many other deficiencies. The scope of the Commission's work was determined by a list of public hearings that was handed to us in early December 2009. At that point, the Commission members had never discussed the possible causes of the crisis, and were never told why those particular subjects were important or why they were chosen as the key issues for a set of hearings that would form the backbone of all the Commission's work. The Commission members did not get together to discuss or decide on the causes of the financial crisis until July 2010, well after it was too late to direct the activities of the staff. The Commission interviewed hundreds of witnesses, and the majority's report is full of statements such as "Smith told the FCIC that . . ." However, unless the meeting was public, the Commissioners were not told that an interview would occur, did not know who was being interviewed, were not encouraged to attend, and, of course, did not have an opportunity to question these sources or understand the contexts in which the quoted statements were made. The Commission majority's report uses these opinions as substitutes for data, which are notably lacking in their report; opinions in general are not worth much, especially in hindsight and when given without opportunity for challenge.

The Commission's authorizing statute required that the Commission report on or before December 15, 2010. The original plan was for us to start seeing drafts of the report in April. We didn't see any drafts until November. We were then given an opportunity to submit comments in writing, but never had an opportunity to go over the wording as a group or to know whether our comments were accepted. We received a complete copy of the majority's report, for the first time, on December 15. It was almost 900 double-spaced pages long. The date for approval of the report was eight days later, on December 23. That is not the way to achieve a bipartisan report or the full agreement of any group that takes the issues seriously.

---

3. Edward Pinto, "Government Housing Policies in the Lead-Up to the Financial Crisis: A Forensic Study," http://www.aei.org/docLib/Government-Housing-Policies-Financial-Crisis-Pinto-102110.pdf.

This dissenting statement is organized as follows: Part I summarizes the main points of the dissent. Part II describes how the growth of subprime and other high-risk mortgages drove the growth of the bubble and weakened financial institutions around the world when these mortgages began to default. Part III outlines in detail the housing policies of the U.S. government that were primarily responsible for the fact that approximately one-half of all U.S. mortgages in 2007 were subprime or otherwise of low quality. Part IV is a brief conclusion.

PART I

Summary

∽

Although there were many contributing factors, the housing bubble of 1997–2007 would not have reached its dizzying heights or lasted as long, nor would the financial crisis of 2008 have ensued, but for the role played by the housing policies of the U.S. government over the course of two administrations. As a result of these policies, by the middle of 2007, there were approximately 27 million subprime and Alt-A mortgages in the U.S. financial system—half of all mortgages outstanding—with an aggregate value of over $4.5 trillion.[1] These were unprecedented numbers, far higher than at any time in the past, and the losses associated with the delinquency and default of these mortgages fully account for the weakness and disruption of the financial system that has become known as the financial crisis.

Most subprime and Alt-A mortgages are high-risk loans. A subprime mortgage is a loan to a borrower who has blemished credit, usually signified by a Fair Isaac Corporation (FICO) credit score lower than 660.[2] Typically, a subprime borrower has failed in the past to meet

---

1. Unless otherwise indicated, all estimates for the number of subprime and Alt-A mortgages outstanding, as well as the use of specific terms such as "loan-to-value ratios" and "delinquency rates," come from research done by Edward Pinto, a resident fellow at the American Enterprise Institute. Pinto is also a consultant to the housing finance industry and a former chief credit officer of Fannie Mae. Much of this work is posted on both my and Pinto's scholar pages at AEI as follows: http://www.aei.org/docLib/Pinto-Sizing-Total-Exposure. pdf, which accounts for all 27 million high-risk loans; http://www.aei.org/docLib/Pinto-Sizing-Total-Federal-Contributions.pdf, which covers the portion of these loans that were held or guaranteed by federal agencies and the four large banks that made these loans under CRA; and http://www.aei.org/docLib/Pinto-High-LTV-Subprime-Alt-A.pdf, which covers the acquisition of these loans by government agencies from the early 1990s. The information in these memoranda is fully cited to original sources. These memoranda were the data exhibits to a Pinto memorandum submitted to the FCIC in January 2010, and revised and updated in March 2010 (collectively, the "Triggers memo").

2. One of the confusing elements of any study of the mortgage markets is the fact that the key definitions have never been fully agreed upon. For many years, Fannie Mae treated as subprime loans only those that it

other financial obligations. Before changes in government policy in the early 1990s, most borrowers with FICO scores below 660 did not qualify as prime borrowers and had difficulty obtaining mortgage credit other than through the Federal Housing Administration, the government's original subprime lender, or through a relatively small number of specialized subprime lenders.

An Alt-A mortgage is one that is deficient by its terms. It may have an adjustable rate, lack documentation about the borrower, require payment of interest only, or be made to an investor in rental housing, not a prospective homeowner. Another key deficiency in many Alt-A mortgages is a high loan-to-value ratio—that is, a low downpayment. A low downpayment for a home may signify the borrower's lack of financial resources, and this lack of "skin in the game" often means a reduced borrower commitment to the home. Until they became subject to HUD's affordable housing requirements, beginning in the early 1990s, Fannie and Freddie seldom acquired loans with these deficiencies.

Given the likelihood that large numbers of subprime and Alt-A mortgages would default once the housing bubble began to deflate in mid-2007—with devastating effects for the U.S. economy and financial system—the key question for the FCIC was to determine why, beginning in the early 1990s, mortgage underwriting standards began to deteriorate so significantly that it was possible to create 27 million subprime and Alt-A mortgages. The Commission never made a serious study of this question, although understanding why and how this happened must be viewed as one of the central questions of the financial crisis.

From the beginning, the Commission's investigation was limited to validating the standard narrative about the financial crisis—that it was caused by deregulation or lack of regulation, weak risk management, predatory lending, unregulated derivatives, and greed on Wall Street. Other hypotheses were either never considered or were treated only superficially. In criticizing the Commission, this statement is not intended to criticize the staff, who worked diligently and effectively under difficult circumstances and did extraordinarily fine work in the limited areas they were directed to cover. The Commission's failures were failures of management.

---

purchased from subprime originators. *Inside Mortgage Finance,* a common source of data on the mortgage market, treated and recorded as subprime only those loans reported as subprime by the originators or by Fannie and Freddie. Other loans were recorded as prime, even if they had credit scores that would have classified them as subprime. However, a FICO credit score of less than 660 is generally regarded as a subprime loan, no matter how originated. That is the standard, for example, used by the Office of the Comptroller of the Currency. In this statement and in Pinto's work on this issue, loans that are classified as subprime by their originators are called "self-denominated" subprime loans, and loans to borrowers with FICO scores of less than 660 are called subprime by characteristic. Fannie and Freddie reported only a very small percentage of their loans as subprime, so, in effect, the subprime loans acquired by Fannie and Freddie should be added to the self-denominated subprime loans originated by others in order to derive something closer to the number and principal amount of the subprime loans outstanding in the financial system at any given time. One of the important elements of Edward Pinto's work was to show that Fannie and Freddie, for many years prior to the financial crisis, were buying loans that should have been classified as subprime because of the borrowers' credit scores and not simply because they were originated by subprime lenders. Fannie and Freddie did not do this until after they were taken over by the federal government. This lack of disclosure on the part of the GSEs appears to have been a factor in the failure of many market observers to foresee the potential severity of the mortgage defaults when the housing bubble deflated in 2007.

1. GOVERNMENT POLICIES RESULTED IN AN UNPRECEDENTED NUMBER OF RISKY MORTGAGES

Three specific government programs were primarily responsible for the growth of subprime and Alt-A mortgages in the U.S. economy between 1992 and 2008 and for the decline in mortgage underwriting standards that ensued.

The GSEs' Affordable Housing Mission

The fact that high-risk mortgages formed almost half of all U.S. mortgages by the middle of 2007 was not a chance event, nor did it just happen that banks and other mortgage originators decided on their own to offer easy credit terms to potential homebuyers beginning in the 1990s.

In 1992, Congress enacted Title XIII of the Housing and Community Development Act of 1992[3] (the GSE Act), legislation intended to give low- and moderate-income[4] borrowers better access to mortgage credit through Fannie Mae and Freddie Mac. This effort, probably stimulated by a desire to increase home ownership, ultimately became a set of regulations that required Fannie and Freddie to reduce the mortgage underwriting standards they used when acquiring loans from originators. As the Senate Committee report said at the time: "The purpose of [the affordable housing] goals is to facilitate the development in both Fannie Mae and Freddie Mac of an ongoing business effort that will be fully integrated in their products, cultures and day-to-day operations to service the mortgage finance needs of low-and-moderate-income persons, racial minorities and inner-city residents."[5] The GSE Act, and its subsequent enforcement by HUD, set in motion a series of changes in the structure of the mortgage market in the United States and, more particularly, the gradual degrading of traditional mortgage underwriting standards. Accordingly, in this dissenting statement, I will refer to the subprime and Alt-A mortgages that were acquired because of the affordable housing (AH) goals, as well as other subprime and Alt-A mortgages, as nontraditional mortgages, or NTMs.

The GSE Act was a radical departure from the original conception of the GSEs as managers of a secondary market in prime mortgages. Fannie Mae was established as a government agency in the New Deal era to buy mortgages from banks and other loan originators, providing them with new funds with which to make additional mortgages. In 1968, Fannie Mae was authorized to sell shares to the public and became a GSE[6]—a shareholder-owned

3. Public Law 102-550, 106 Stat. 3672, H.R. 5334, enacted October 28, 1992.

4. Low income is usually defined as 80 percent of area median income (AMI), and moderate income as 100 percent of AMI.

5. Report of the Committee on Banking, Housing and Urban Affairs, United States Senate, to accompany S. 2733. Report 102-282, May 15, 1992, pp. 34–35.

6. Fannie and Freddie were considered to be government sponsored enterprises because they had been chartered by Congress and were given various privileges (such as exemption from the Securities Act of 1933

company with a government mission to maintain a liquid secondary market in mortgages. Freddie Mac was chartered by Congress as another GSE in 1970. Fannie and Freddie carried out their mission effectively until the early 1990s, and in the process established conservative lending standards for the mortgages they were willing to purchase, including elements such as downpayments of 10 to 20 percent, and minimum credit standards for borrowers.

The GSE Act, however, created a new "mission" for Fannie Mae and Freddie Mac—a responsibility to support affordable housing—and authorized HUD to establish and administer what was in effect a mortgage quota system in which a certain percentage of all Fannie and Freddie mortgage purchases had to be loans to low- and moderate-income (LMI) borrowers—defined as persons with income at or below the median income in a particular area—or to borrowers living in certain low-income communities. These AH goals put Fannie and Freddie into direct competition with the FHA, which was then and is today an agency within HUD that functions as the federal government's principal subprime lender.

Over the next fifteen years, HUD consistently enhanced and enlarged the AH goals. In the GSE Act, Congress had initially specified that 30 percent of the GSEs' mortgage purchases meet the AH goals. This was increased to 42 percent in 1995 and 50 percent in 2000. By 2008, the main LMI goal was 56 percent, and a special affordable subgoal had been added requiring that 27 percent of the loans acquired by the GSEs be made to borrowers who were at or below 80 percent of area median income (AMI). Table 10, page 71, shows that Fannie and Freddie met the goals in almost every year between 1996 and 2008.

There are very little data available concerning Fannie and Freddie's acquisitions of subprime and Alt-A loans in the early 1990s, so it is difficult to estimate the GSEs' year-by-year acquisitions of these loans immediately after the AH goals went into effect. However, Pinto estimates the total value of these purchases at approximately $4.1 trillion (see table 7, page 65). As shown in table 1, on June 30, 2008, immediately prior to the onset of the financial crisis, the GSEs held or had guaranteed 12 million subprime and Alt-A loans. This was 37 percent of their total mortgage exposure of 32 million loans, which, in turn, was approximately 58 percent of the 55 million mortgages outstanding in the United States on that date. Fannie and Freddie, accordingly, were by far the dominant players in the U.S. mortgage market before the financial crisis, and their underwriting standards largely set the standards for the rest of the mortgage financing industry.

The Community Reinvestment Act

In 1995, the regulations under the Community Reinvestment Act[7] were tightened. As initially adopted in 1977, the CRA and its associated regulations required only that insured

---

and the Securities Exchange Act of 1934) and a line of credit at the Treasury that signaled a special degree of government support. As a result, the capital markets (which continued to call them "Agencies") assumed that, in the event of financial difficulties, the government would stand behind them. This implied government backing gave them access to funding that was lower cost than any AAA borrower and often only a few basis points over the applicable Treasury rate.

7. Pub.L. 95-128, Title VIII of the Housing and Community Development Act of 1977, 91 Stat. 1147, 12 U.S.C. § 2901 *et seq.*

TABLE 1
ENTITIES HOLDING CREDIT RISK OF SUBPRIME AND OTHER HIGH-RISK MORTGAGES

Entity	No. of Subprime and Alt-A Loans	Unpaid Principal Amount
Fannie Mae and Freddie Mac	12 million	$1.8 trillion
FHA and other Federal*	5 million	$0.6 trillion
CRA and HUD Programs	2.2 million	$0.3 trillion
Total Federal Government	**19.2 million**	**$2.7 trillion**
Other (including subprime and Alt-A PMBS issued by Countrywide, Wall Street and others)	7.8 million	$1.9 trillion
Total	**27 million**	**$4.6 trillion**

SOURCE: See Edward Pinto's analysis in Exhibit 2 to the Triggers Memo, April 21, 2010, p. 4, http://www.aei.org/docLib/Pinto-Sizing-Total-Federal-Contributions.pdf.
NOTE: * = Includes Veterans Administration, Federal Home Loan Banks, and others.

banks and S&Ls reach out to low-income borrowers in communities they served. The new regulations, made effective in 1995, for the first time required insured banks and S&Ls to demonstrate that they were actually making loans in low-income communities and to low-income borrowers.[8] A qualifying CRA loan was one made to a borrower at or below 80 percent of the AMI and thus was similar to the loans that Fannie and Freddie were required to buy under HUD's AH goals.

In 2007, the National Community Reinvestment Coalition (NCRC), an umbrella organization for community activist organizations, reported that between 1997 and 2007 banks that were seeking regulatory approval for mergers committed, in agreements with community groups, to make over $4.5 trillion in CRA loans.[9] A substantial portion of these commitments appear to have been converted into mortgage loans and thus would have contributed substantially to the number of subprime and other high-risk loans outstanding in 2008. For this reason, they deserved Commission investigation and analysis. Unfortunately, as outlined in Part III, this was not done.

Accordingly, the GSE Act put Fannie and Freddie, FHA, and the banks that were seeking CRA loans into competition for the same mortgages—loans to borrowers at or below the applicable AMI.

HUD's Best Practices Initiative

In 1994, HUD added another group to this list when it set up a Best Practices Initiative, to which 117 members of the Mortgage Bankers Association eventually adhered. As shown later, this program was explicitly intended to encourage a reduction in underwriting standards so as to increase access by low-income borrowers to mortgage credit. Countrywide

---

8. http://www.fdic.gov/regulations/laws/rules/2000-6500.html.
9. See http://www.community-wealth.org/_pdfs/articles-publications/cdfis/report-silver-brown.pdf.

was by far the largest member of this group and by the early 2000s was also competing, along with others, for the same NTMs sought by Fannie and Freddie, FHA, and the banks under the CRA.

With all these entities seeking the same loans, it was not likely that all of them would find enough borrowers who could meet the traditional mortgage lending standards that Fannie and Freddie had established. It also created ideal conditions for a decline in underwriting standards, since every one of these competing entities was seeking NTMs not for purposes of profit but in order to meet an obligation imposed by the government. The obvious way to meet this obligation was simply to reduce the underwriting standards that impeded compliance with the government's requirements.

Indeed, by the early 1990s, traditional underwriting standards had come to be seen as an obstacle to home ownership by LMI families. In a 1991 Senate Banking Committee hearing, Gail Cincotta, a highly respected supporter of low-income lending, observed that "lenders will respond to the most conservative standards unless [Fannie Mae and Freddie Mac] are aggressive and convincing in their efforts to expand historically narrow underwriting."[10]

In this light, it appears that Congress set out deliberately in the GSE Act not only to change the culture of the GSEs, but also to set up a mechanism that would reduce traditional underwriting standards over time, so that home ownership would be more accessible to LMI borrowers. For example, the legislation directed the GSEs to study "the implications of implementing underwriting standards that—(A) establish a downpayment requirement for mortgagors of 5 percent or less;[11] (B) allow the use of cash on hand as a source of downpayments; and (C) approve borrowers who have a credit history of delinquencies if the borrower can demonstrate a satisfactory credit history for at least the 12-month period ending on the date of the application for the mortgage."[12] None of these elements was part of traditional mortgage underwriting standards as understood at the time.

I have been unable to find any studies by Fannie or Freddie in response to this congressional direction, but HUD treated these cues as a mandate to use the AH goals as a mechanism for eroding the traditional standards. HUD was very explicit about this, as shown in Part II. In the end, the goal was accomplished by gradually expanding the requirements and enlarging the AH goals over succeeding years, so that the only way Fannie and Freddie could meet the AH goals was by purchasing increasing numbers of subprime and Alt-A mortgages, and particularly mortgages with low or no downpayments. Because the GSEs were the dominant players in the mortgage market, their purchases also put competitive pressure on the other entities that were subject to government control—FHA and the banks under CRA—to reach deeper into subprime lending in order to find the mortgages they needed to comply with their own government requirements. This was also true of the

---

10. Allen Fishbein, "Filling the Half-Empty Glass: The Role of Community Advocacy in Redefining the Public Responsibilities of Government-Sponsored Housing Enterprises," chapter 7 of *Organizing Access to Capital: Advocacy and the Democratization of Financial Institutions,* 2003, Gregory Squires, editor.

11. At that time, the GSEs' minimum downpayment was 5 percent and was accompanied by conservative underwriting. The congressional request was to break through that limitation.

12. GSE Act, Section 1354(a).

mortgage banks—the largest of which was Countrywide—that were bound to promote affordable housing through HUD's Best Practices Initiative.

By 2008, the result of these government programs was an unprecedented number of subprime and other high-risk mortgages in the U.S. financial system. Table 1 shows which agencies or firms were holding the credit risk of these mortgages—or had distributed risk to investors through mortgage-backed securities—immediately before the financial crisis began. As table 1 makes clear, government agencies, or private institutions acting under government direction, either held or had guaranteed 19.2 million of the NTM loans that were outstanding at that point. By contrast, about 7.8 million NTMs had been distributed to investors through the issuance of private mortgage-backed securities, or PMBS,[13] primarily by private issuers such as Countrywide and other subprime lenders.

The fact that the credit risk of two-thirds of all the NTMs in the financial system was held by the government or by entities acting under government control demonstrates the central role of the government's policies in the development of the 1997–2007 housing bubble, the mortgage meltdown that occurred when the bubble deflated, and the financial crisis and recession that ensued. Similarly, the fact that only 7.8 million NTMs were held by investors and financial institutions in the form of PMBS shows that this group of NTMs was less important as a cause of the financial crisis than the government's role. The Commission majority's report focuses almost entirely on the 7.8 million PMBS; this is an example of its determination to ignore the government's role in the financial crisis.

To be sure, the government's efforts to increase home ownership through the AH goals succeeded. Home ownership rates in the United States increased from approximately 64 percent in 1994 (where rates had stayed for thirty years) to over 69 percent in 2004.[14] Almost everyone in and out of government was pleased with this—a long-term goal of U.S. housing policy—until the true costs became clear with the collapse of the housing bubble in 2007. Then, an elaborate process of shifting the blame began.

2. THE GREAT HOUSING BUBBLE AND ITS EFFECTS

Figure 1 (page 16), based on the data of Robert J. Shiller, shows the dramatic growth of the 1997–2007 housing bubble in the United States. By mid-2007, home prices in the United States had increased substantially for ten years. The growth in real-dollar terms had been almost 90 percent, ten times greater than any other housing bubble in modern times. As discussed below, there is good reason to believe that the 1997–2007 bubble grew larger and extended longer in time than previous bubbles because of the government's housing

---

13. In the process known as "securitization," securities backed by a pool of mortgages (mortgage-backed securities, or MBS) and issued by private-sector firms were known as "private label securities" (distinguishing them from securities issued by the GSEs or Ginnie Mae) or private MBS (PMBS).

14. Census Bureau data.

FIGURE 1
THE BUBBLE ACCORDING TO SHILLER

A History of Home Values

The Yale economist Robert J. Shiller created an index of American housing prices going back to 1890. It is based on sale prices of standard existing houses, not new construction, to track the value of housing as an investment over time. It presents housing values in consistent terms over 116 years, factoring out the effects of inflation.

The 1890 benchmark is 100 on the chart. If a standard house sold in 1890 for $100,000 (inflation-adjusted to today's dollars), an equivalent standard house would have sold for $66,000 in 1920 (66 on the index scale) and $199,000 in 2006 (199 on the index scale, or 99 percent higher than 1890).

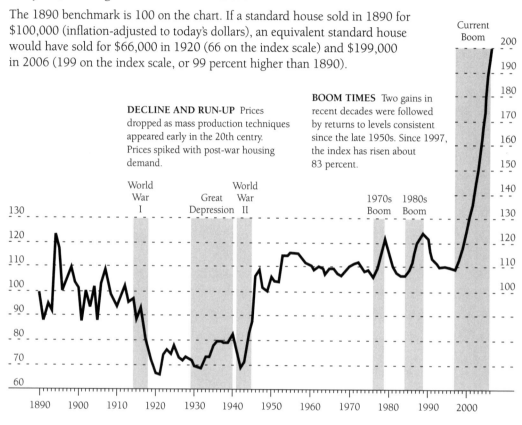

SOURCE: Robert J. Shiller, *Irrational Exuberance,* 2nd edition, Princeton University Press, 2006. Graph courtesy of the *New York Times.*

policies, which artificially increased the demand for housing by funneling more money into the housing market than would have been available if traditional lending standards had been maintained and the government had not promoted the growth of subprime lending.

That the 1997–2007 bubble lasted about twice as long as the prior housing bubbles is significant in itself. Mortgage quality declines as a housing bubble grows and originators try to structure mortgages that will allow buyers to meet monthly payments for more expensive homes; the fact that the most recent bubble was so long-lived was an important element in its ultimate destructiveness when it deflated. Why did this bubble last so long? Housing bubbles deflate when delinquencies and defaults begin to appear in unusual numbers. Investors and creditors realize that the risks of a collapse are mounting. One by one, investors cash in and leave. Eventually, the bubble tops out, those who are still in the game run for the doors, and a deflation in prices sets in. Generally, in the past, this process has taken three or four years. In the case of the most recent bubble, it took ten. The reason for this longevity is that one major participant in the market was not motivated by profit and was not worried about the risks to itself or to those it was controlling. It was the U.S. government, pursuing a social policy—increasing homeownership by making mortgage credit available to low- and moderate-income borrowers—and requiring the agencies and financial institutions it controlled or could influence through regulation to keep pumping money into housing long after the bubble, left to itself, would have deflated.

Economists have been vigorously debating whether the monetary policy of the Federal Reserve System (the Fed) in the early 2000s caused the bubble by keeping interest rates too low for too long. Naturally enough, Ben Bernanke and Alan Greenspan have argued that the Fed was not at fault. On the other hand, John Taylor, author of the Taylor rule, contends that the Fed's violation of the Taylor rule was the principal cause of the bubble. Raghuram Rajan, a professor at the University of Chicago Booth School of Business, argues that the Fed's low interest rates caused the bubble, but that the Fed actually followed this policy in order to combat unemployment rather than deflation.[15] Other theories blame huge inflows of funds from emerging markets or from countries that were recycling the dollars they received from trade surpluses with the United States. These debates, however, may be missing the point. It doesn't matter where the funds that built the bubble actually originated; the important question is why they were transformed into NTMs that were prone to failure as soon as the great bubble deflated.

Figure 2 illustrates clearly that the 1997–2007 bubble was built on a foundation of 27 million subprime and Alt-A mortgages and shows the relationship between the cumulative growth in the dollar amount of NTMs and the growth of the bubble over time. It includes both GSE and CRA contributions to the number of outstanding NTMs above the normal baseline of 30 percent,[16] and estimated CRA lending under the merger-related commitments of the four large banks—Bank of America, Wells Fargo, Citibank and JPMorgan Chase—that, with their predecessors, made most of the commitments. As noted above, these commitments were made in connection with applications to federal regulators for approvals of mergers or acquisitions. The dollar amounts involved were taken from a 2007 report by the NCRC[17] and adjusted for announced loans and likely rates of lending. The

---

15. See Bernanke testimony before the FCIC, September 2, 2010; Alan Greenspan, "The Crisis," second draft, March 9, 2010; Taylor, testimony before the FCIC on October 20, 2009; John B. Taylor, *Getting Off Track*, Hoover Institution Press, 2009; and Raghuram Rajan, *Fault Lines: How Hidden Fractures Still Threaten the World Economy*, Princeton University Press, 2010, pp. 108–110.

16. It appears that the GSEs' normal intake of mortgages included about 30 percent that were made to borrowers who were at or below the median income in the area in which they lived and were thus eligible for AH credit. It was only when the AH goals rose above this level, beginning in 1995, that government policy required the GSEs to acquire more AH qualifying loans than they would have purchased as a matter of course. In the case of the CRA contributions, the baseline is 1992 and includes the commitments made by the four largest banks and their predecessors listed in the NCRC report, adjusted for the loans actually announced by the banks after that date.

17. In 2007, the National Community Reinvestment Coalition published a report on the principal amount of CRA loans that banks had committed to make in connection with merger applications. The report claimed that these commitments exceeded $4.5 trillion. The original report was removed from the NCRC's website but

FIGURE 2

THE EFFECT OF GOVERNMENT POLICIES ON THE GROWTH OF THE BUBBLE

**GSE Affordable Housing Purchases, CRA Production, and Self-Denominated
Subprime Production in Relation to U.S. House Prices (1993 = 100)**

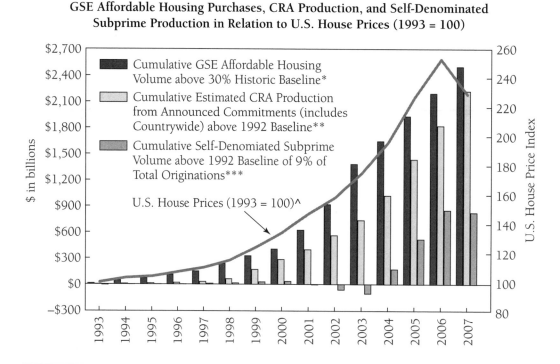

SOURCES: * = HUD; ** = NCRC and Edward Pinto; *** = Inside Mortgage Finance; ^ = S&P/Case-Shiller U.S. Index.

cumulative estimated CRA production line also includes almost $1 trillion in NTM lending by Countrywide Financial under HUD's Best Practices Initiative.[18]

It is not true that every bubble—even a large bubble—has the potential to cause a financial crisis when it deflates. This is clear in table 2, prepared by Professor Dwight Jaffee of the Haas Business School at the University of California, Berkeley. The table shows that in other developed countries—many of which also had large bubbles during the 1997–2007 period—the losses associated with mortgage delinquencies and defaults when these bubbles deflated were far lower than the losses suffered in the United States when the 1997–2007 deflated.

The underlying reasons for the outcomes in Professor Jaffee's data were provided in testimony before the Senate Banking Committee in September 2010 by Dr. Michael Lea, Director of the Corky McMillin Center for Real Estate at San Diego State University:

> The default and foreclosure experience of the U.S. market has been far worse than
> in other countries. Serious default rates remain less than 3 percent in all other

---

can still be found at http://www.community-wealth.org/_pdfs/articles-publications/cdfis/report-silver-brown.pdf. A portion of these commitments were in fact fulfilled through CRA qualifying loans. A full discussion of these commitments and the number of loans made pursuant to them is contained in part III.

18. See note 79, part III.

TABLE 2
TROUBLED MORTGAGES, WESTERN EUROPE AND THE UNITED STATES

	≥ 3 Month Arrears %	Impaired or Doubtful %	Foreclosures	Year
Belgium	0.46%			2009
Denmark	0.53%			2009
France		0.93%		2008
Ireland	3.32%			2009
Italy		3.00%		2008
Portugal	1.17%			2009
Spain		3.04%	0.24%	2009
Sweden		1.00%		2009
UK	2.44%		0.19%	2009
U.S. All Loans	9.47%		4.58%	2009
U.S. Prime	6.73%		3.31%	2009
U.S. Subprime	25.26%		15.58%	2009

SOURCES: Dwight M. Jaffee, "Reforming the U.S. Mortgage Market Through Private Market Incentives," Paper prepared for presentation at "Past, Present and Future of the Government Sponsored Enterprises," Federal Reserve Bank of St. Louis, Nov 17, 2010, Table 4. Data from European Mortgage Federation (2010) and Mortgage Bankers Association for U.S. Data.

countries and less than 1 percent in Australia and Canada. Of the countries in this survey only Ireland, Spain and the UK have seen a significant increase in mortgage default during the crisis.

There are several factors responsible for this result. First subprime lending was rare or non-existent outside of the U.S. The only country with a significant subprime share was the UK (a peak of 8 percent of mortgages in 2006). Subprime accounted for 5 percent of mortgages in Canada, less than 2 percent in Australia and negligible proportions elsewhere.

. . . [T]here was far less "risk layering" or offering limited documentation loans to subprime borrowers with little or no downpayment. There was little "no doc" lending…the proportion of loans with little or no downpayment was less than the U.S. and the decline in house prices in most countries was also less . . . [L]oans in other developed countries are with recourse and lenders routinely go after borrowers for deficiency judgments.[19]

The fact that the destructiveness of the 1997–2007 bubble came from its composition—the number of NTMs it contained—rather than its size is also illustrated by data on foreclosure starts published by the Mortgage Bankers Association (MBA).[20] These data allow a comparison between the foreclosure starts that have thus far come out of the 1997–2007

19. Dr. Michael J. Lea, testimony before the Subcommittee on Security and International Trade and Finance of the Senate Banking Committee, September 29, 2010, p. 6.

20. Mortgage Bankers Association National Delinquency Survey.

bubble and the foreclosure starts in the two most recent housing bubbles (1977–1979 and 1985–1989) shown in figure 1. After the housing bubble that ended in 1979, when almost all mortgages were prime loans of the traditional type, foreclosure starts in the ensuing downturn reached a high point of only 0.87 percent in 1983. After the next bubble, which ended in 1989 and in which a high proportion of the loans were the traditional type, foreclosure starts reached a high of 1.32 percent in 1994. However, after the collapse of the 1997–2007 bubble—in which half of all mortgages were NTMs—foreclosure starts reached the unprecedented level (thus far) of 5.3 percent in 2009. And this was true despite numerous government and bank efforts to prevent or delay foreclosures.

All the foregoing data are significant for a proper analysis of the role of government policy and NTMs in the financial crisis. What they suggest is that whatever effect low interest rates or money flows from abroad might have had in creating the great U.S. housing bubble, the deflation of that bubble need not have been destructive. It wasn't just the size of the bubble; it was also the content. The enormous delinquency rates in the United States (see table 3 on page 21) were not replicated elsewhere, primarily because other developed countries did not have the numbers of NTMs that were present in the U.S. financial system when the bubble deflated. As shown in later sections of this dissent, these mortgage defaults were translated into huge housing price declines and from there—through the PMBS they were holding—into actual or apparent financial weakness in the banks and other firms that held these securities.

Accordingly, if the 1997–2007 housing bubble had not been seeded with an unprecedented number of NTMs, it is likely that the financial crisis would never have occurred.

3. Delinquency Rates on Nontraditional Mortgages

NTMs are nontraditional because, for many years before the government adopted affordable housing policies, mortgages of this kind constituted only a small portion of all housing loans in the United States.[21] The traditional residential mortgage—known as a conventional mortgage—generally had a fixed rate, often for fifteen or thirty years, a downpayment of 10 to 20 percent, and was made to a borrower who had a job, a steady income, and a good credit record. Before the GSE Act, even subprime loans, although made to borrowers with impaired credit, often involved substantial downpayments or existing equity in homes.[22]

Table 3 shows the delinquency rates of the NTMs that were outstanding on June 30, 2008. The grayed area contains virtually all the NTMs. The contrast in quality, based on delinquency rates, between these loans and Fannie and Freddie prime loans in lines 9 and 10 is clear.

---

21. See Pinto, "Government Housing Policies in the Lead-Up to the Financial Crisis: A Forensic Study," November 4, 2010, p. 58, http://www.aei.org/docLib/Government-Housing-Policies-Financial-Crisis-Pinto-102110.pdf.

22. Id., p. 42.

TABLE 3
DELINQUENCY RATES ON NONTRADITIONAL MORTGAGES

Loan Type	Estimated # of Loans	Total Delinquency Rate (30+ Days and in Foreclosure)
1. High Rate Subprime (including Fannie/Freddie private MBS holdings)	6.7 million	45.0%
2. Option Arm	1.1 million	30.5%
3. Alt-A (inc. Fannie/Freddie/FHLBs private MBS holdings)	2.4 million[†]	23.0%
4. Fannie Subprime/Atl-A/Nonprime	6.6 million	17.3%
5. Freddie Subprime/Alt-A/Nonprime	4.1 million	13.8%
6. Government	4.8 million	13.5%
Subtotal # of Loans	**25.7 million**	
7. Non-Agency Jumbo Prime	9.4 million[‡]	6.8%
8. Non-Agency Conforming Prime*		5.6%
9. Fannie Prime **	11.2 million	2.6%
10. Freddie Prime***	8.7 million	2.0%
Total # of Loans	**55 million**	

SOURCES: Pinto, "Government Housing Policies in the Lead-up to the Financial Crisis: A Forensic Study," November 4, 2010, chart 53, http://www.aei.org/docLib/Government-Housing-Policies-Financial-Crisis-Pinto-102110.pdf.
Total delinquency data sources: 1, 2, 3, 6, 7 & 8: Lender Processing Services, LPS Mortgage Monitor, June 2009; 4 & 9: Based on Fannie Mae 2009 2Q Credit Supplement. Converted from a serious delinquency rate (90+ days & in foreclosure) to an estimated Total Delinquency Rate (30+ days and in foreclosure); 5 & 10: Based on Freddie Mac 2009 2Q Financial Results Supplement. Converted from a serious delinquency rate (90+ days & in foreclosure) to an estimated Total Delinquency Rate (30+ days and in foreclosure).
NOTES: * = Includes an estimated 1 million subprime (FICO <660) that were (i) not high rate and (ii) non-prime CRA and HUD Best Practices Initiative loans. These are included in the "CRA and HUD Programs" line in Table 1.
** = Excludes Fannie subprime/Alt-A/nonprime.
*** = Excludes Freddie subprime/Alt-A/nonprime.
† = Excludes loans owned or securitized by Fannie and Freddie.
‡ = Non-agency jumbo prime and conforming prime counted together.

4. THE ORIGIN AND GROWTH OF SUBPRIME PMBS

It was only in 2002 that the market for subprime PMBS—that is, private mortgage-backed securities backed by subprime loans or other NTMs—reached $100 billion. In that year, the top five issuers were GMAC-RFC ($11.5 billion), Lehman ($10.6 billion), CS First Boston ($10.5 billion), Bank of America ($10.4 billion) and Ameriquest ($9 billion).[23] The issuances of PMBS that year totaled $134 billion, of which $43 billion in PMBS was issued by Wall Street financial institutions. In subsequent years, as the market grew, Wall Street institutions fell behind the major subprime issuers, so that by 2005—the biggest year for subprime

---

23. Inside Mortgage Finance, *The 2009 Mortgage Market Statistical Annual—Vol. II*, p. 143.

PMBS issuance—only Lehman was among the top five issuers, and Wall Street issuers as a group were only 27 percent of the $507 billion in total PMBS issuance in that year.[24]

One of the many myths about the financial crisis is that Wall Street banks led the way into subprime lending and the GSEs followed. The Commission majority's report adopts this idea as a way of explaining why Fannie and Freddie acquired so many NTMs. This notion simply does not align with the facts. Not only were Wall Street institutions small factors in the subprime PMBS market, but well before 2002, Fannie and Freddie were much bigger players than the entire PMBS market in the business of acquiring NTM and other subprime loans. Table 7, page 65, shows that Fannie and Freddie had already acquired at least $701 billion in NTMs by 2001. Obviously, the GSEs did not have to follow anyone into NTM or subprime lending; they were already the dominant players in that market before 2002. Table 7 also shows that in 2002, when the entire PMBS market was $134 billion, Fannie and Freddie acquired $206 billion in whole subprime mortgages and $368 billion in other NTMs, demonstrating again that the GSEs were no strangers to risky lending well before the PMBS market began to develop.

Further evidence about which firms were first into subprime or NTM lending is provided by Fannie's 2002 10-K. This disclosure document reports that 14 percent of Fannie's credit obligations (either in portfolio or guaranteed) had FICO credit scores below 660 as of December 31, 2000, 16 percent as of the end of 2001, and 17 percent as of the end of 2002.[25] So Fannie and Freddie were active and major buyers of subprime loans in years when the PMBS market had total issuances of only $55 billion (2000) and $94 billion (2001). In other words, it would be more accurate to say that Wall Street followed Fannie and Freddie into subprime lending rather than vice versa. At the same time, the GSEs' purchases of subprime whole loans throughout the 1990s stimulated the growth of the subprime lending industry, which ultimately became the mainstay of the subprime PMBS market in the 2000s.

2005 was the biggest year for PMBS subprime issuances, and Ameriquest ($54 billion) and Countrywide ($38 billion) were the two largest issuers in the top twenty-five. These numbers were still small in relation to what Fannie and Freddie had been buying since data became available in 1997. The total in table 7 for Fannie and Freddie between 1997 and 2007 is approximately $1.5 trillion for subprime loans and over $4 trillion for all NTMs as a group.

Because subprime PMBS were rich in NTM loans eligible for credit under HUD's AH goals, Fannie and Freddie were also the largest individual purchasers of subprime PMBS from 2002 to 2006, acquiring 33 percent of the total issuances, or $579 billion.[26] In table 3 (page 21), which organizes mortgages by delinquency rate, these purchases are included in line 1, which had the highest rate of delinquency. These were self-denominated subprime—designated as subprime by the lender when originated—and thus had low FICO scores and usually a higher interest rate than prime loans; many also had low downpayments and were subject to other deficiencies.

---

24. Id., p. 140.

25. 2003 10-K, table 33, p. 84 http://www.sec.gov/Archives/edgar/data/310522/000095013303001151/w84239e10vk.htm#031.

26. See table 3 of "High LTV, Subprime and Alt-A Originations Over the Period 1992–2007 and Fannie, Freddie, FHA and VA's Role" found at http://www.aei.org/docLib/Pinto-High-LTV-Subprime-Alt-A.pdf.

Ultimately, HUD's policies were responsible for both the poor quality of the subprime and Alt-A mortgages that backed the PMBS and for the enormous size to which this market grew. This was true not only because Fannie and Freddie stimulated the growth of that market through their purchases of PMBS, but also because the huge inflow of government or government-directed funds into the housing market turned what would have been a normal housing bubble into a bubble of unprecedented size and duration. This enabled and encouraged unprecedented growth in the PMBS market in two ways.

First, the gradual increase of the AH goals, the competition between the GSEs and the FHA, the effect of HUD's Best Practices Initiative, and bank lending under the CRA ensured a continuing flow of funds into weaker and weaker mortgages. This had the effect of extending the life of the housing bubble as well as increasing its size. The growth of the bubble, in turn, disguised the weakness of the subprime mortgages it contained; as housing prices rose, subprime borrowers who might otherwise have defaulted were able to refinance their mortgages, using the equity that had developed in their homes solely through rising home prices. Without the continuous infusion of government or government-directed funds, delinquencies and defaults would have begun showing up within a year or two, bringing the subprime PMBS market to a halt. Instead, the bubble lasted ten years, permitting the market to grow until it reached almost $2 trillion.

Second, as housing prices rose in the bubble, it was necessary for borrowers to seek riskier mortgages in order to afford the monthly payments on more expensive homes. This gave rise to new and riskier forms of mortgage debt, such as option-adjustable-rate mortgages (ARMs) (resulting in negative amortization) and interest-only mortgages. Mortgages of this kind could be suitable for some borrowers, but not for those who were only eligible for subprime loans. Nevertheless, subprime loans were necessary for PMBS, because they generally bore higher interest rates and thus could support the yields that investors were expecting. As subprime loans were originated, Fannie and Freddie were willing consumers of those that might meet the AH goals; moreover, because of their lower cost of funds, they were able to buy the "best of the worst," the highest quality among the NTMs on offer. These factors—the need for higher yielding loans and the ability of Fannie and Freddie to pay up for the loans they wanted—drove private sector issuers further out on the risk curve as they sought to meet the demands of investors who were seeking exposure to subprime PMBS. From the investors' perspective, as long as the bubble kept growing, PMBS were offering the high yields associated with risk but were not showing commensurate numbers of delinquencies and defaults.

5. WHAT WAS KNOWN ABOUT NTMs PRIOR TO THE CRISIS?

Virtually everyone who testified before the Commission agreed that the financial crisis was initiated by the mortgage meltdown that began when the housing bubble began to deflate in 2007. None of these witnesses, however, including the academics consulted by the Commission, the representatives of the rating agencies, the officers of financial institutions that were ultimately endangered by the mortgage downdraft, the regulators and supervisors of financial institutions, and even the renowned investor Warren Buffett,[27] seems to have understood the dimensions of the NTM problem or recognized its significance before the bubble deflated. The Commission majority's report notes that "there were warning signs." There always are, if one searches for them; they are most visible in hindsight, in which the Commission majority, and many of the opinions it cites for this proposition, happily engaged. However, as Michael Lewis's acclaimed book *The Big Short* showed so vividly, very few people in the financial world were actually willing to bet money—even at enormously favorable odds—that the bubble would burst with huge losses. Most seem to have assumed that NTMs were present in the financial system, but not in unusually large numbers.

Even today, there are few references in the media to the number of NTMs that had accumulated in the U.S. financial system before the meltdown began. Yet this is by far the most important fact about the financial crisis. None of the other factors offered by the Commission majority to explain the crisis—lack of regulation, poor regulatory and risk management foresight, Wall Street greed and compensation policies, systemic risk caused by credit default swaps, excessive liquidity and easy credit—do so as plausibly as the failure of a large percentage of the 27 million NTMs that existed in the financial system in 2007.

It appears that market participants were unprepared for the destructiveness of this bubble's collapse because of a chronic lack of information about the composition of the mortgage market. In September 2007, for example, after the deflation of the bubble had begun, and various financial firms were beginning to encounter capital and liquidity difficulties, two Lehman Brothers analysts issued a highly detailed report entitled "Who Owns Residential Credit Risk?"[28] In the tables associated with the report, they estimated the total unpaid principal balance of subprime and Alt-A mortgages outstanding at $2.4 trillion, about half the actual number at the time. Based on this assessment, when they applied a stress scenario in which housing prices declined about 30 percent, they still found that "[t]he aggregate losses in the residential mortgage market under the 'stressed' housing conditions could be about $240 billion, which is manageable, assuming it materializes over a five- to six-year horizon." In the end, of course, the losses were much larger and were recognized under mark-to-market accounting almost immediately, rather than over a five- to six-year period. But the failure of these two analysts to recognize the sheer size of the subprime and Alt-A market, even as late as 2007, is the important point.

Along with most other observers, the Lehman analysts were not aware of the true composition of the mortgage market in 2007. Under the "stressed" housing conditions they applied, they projected that the GSEs would suffer aggregate losses of $9.5 billion (net of mortgage insurance coverage) and that their guarantee fee income would be more than sufficient to cover these losses. Based on known losses and projections recently made by the Federal Housing Finance Agency (FHFA), the GSEs' credit losses alone could total $350

27. See Buffett, testimony before the FCIC, June 2, 2010.
28. Vikas Shilpiekandula and Olga Gorodetski, "Who Owns Residental Credit Risk?" *Lehman Brothers Fixed Income U.S. Securitized Products Research*, September 7, 2007.

billion—more than thirty-five times the Lehman analysts' September 2007 estimate. The analysts could only make such a colossal error if they did not realize that 37 percent—or $1.65 trillion—of the GSEs' credit risk portfolio consisted of subprime and Alt-A loans (see table 1, page 13) or that these weak loans would account for about 75 percent of the GSEs' default losses over 2007–2010.[29] It is also instructive to compare the Lehman analysts' estimate that the 2006 vintage of subprime loans would suffer lifetime losses of 19 percent under "stressed" conditions to other, later, more informed estimates. In early 2010, for example, Moody's made a similar estimate for the 2006 vintage and projected a 38 percent loss rate after the 30 percent decline in housing prices had actually occurred.[30]

The Lehman loss rate projection suggests that the analysts did not have an accurate estimate of the number of NTMs actually outstanding in 2006. Indeed, I have not found any studies in the period before the financial crisis in which anyone—scholar or financial analyst—actually seemed to understand how many NTMs were in the financial system at the time. It was only after the financial crisis, when Edward Pinto began gathering this information from various unrelated and disparate sources that the total number of NTMs in the financial markets became clear. As a result, all loss projections before Pinto's work were bound to be faulty.

Much of the Commission majority's report, which criticizes firms, regulators, corporate executives, risk managers, and ratings agency analysts for failure to perceive the losses that lay ahead, is sheer hindsight. It appears that information about the composition of the mortgage market was simply not available when the bubble began to deflate. The Commission never attempted a serious study of what was known about the composition of the mortgage market in 2007, apparently satisfied simply to blame market participants for failing to understand the risks that lay before them, without trying to understand what information was actually available.

The mortgage market is studied constantly by thousands of analysts, academics, regulators, traders, and investors. How could all of these people have missed something as important as the actual number of NTMs outstanding? Most market participants appear to have assumed in the bubble years that Fannie and Freddie continued to adhere to the same conservative underwriting policies they had previously pursued. Until Fannie and Freddie were required to meet HUD's AH goals, they rarely acquired subprime or other low-quality mortgages. Indeed, the very definition of a traditional prime mortgage was a loan that Fannie and Freddie would buy. Lesser loans were rejected and were ultimately insured by FHA or made by a relatively small group of subprime originators and investors.

Although anyone who followed HUD's AH regulations, and thought through their implications, would have realized that Fannie and Freddie must have been shifting their buying activities to low-quality loans, few people had incentives to uncover the new buying pattern. Investors believed that there was no significant risk in MBS backed by Fannie

29. Fannie Mae, 2010 Second Quarter Credit Supplement, http://www.fanniemae.com/ir/pdf/sec/2010/q2credit_summary.pdf.

30. "Moody's Projects Losses of Almost Half of Original Balance from 2007 Subprime Mortgage Securities," http://seekingalpha.com/article/182556-moodys-projects-losses-of-almost-half-of-original-balance-from-2007-subprime-mortgage-securities.

and Freddie, since they were thought (correctly, as it turns out) to be implicitly backed by the federal government. In addition, the GSEs were exempted by law from having to file information with the SEC—they agreed to file voluntarily in 2002—leaving them free from disclosure obligations and questions from analysts about the quality of their mortgages.

When Fannie voluntarily began filing reports with the SEC in 2003, it disclosed that 16 percent of its credit obligations on mortgages had FICO scores of less than 660—the common definition of a subprime loan. There are occasionally questions about whether a FICO score of 660 is the appropriate dividing line between prime and subprime loans. The federal bank regulators use 660 as the dividing line,[31] and in the credit supplement it published for the first time with its 2008 10-K, Fannie included loans with FICO scores below 660 to disclose its exposure to loans that were other than prime. As of December 31, 2008, borrowers with a FICO score of less than 660 had a serious delinquency rate about four times that for borrowers with a FICO score equal to or greater than 660 (6.74 percent compared to 1.72 percent).[32] Fannie did not point out in its filing that a FICO score of less than 660 was considered a subprime loan. Although at the end of 2005 Fannie was exposed to $311 billion in subprime loans, it reported in its 2005 10-K (not filed with the SEC until May 2, 2007) that "the percentage of our single-family mortgage credit book of business consisting of subprime mortgage loans or structured Fannie Mae MBS backed by subprime mortgage loans was *not material* as of December 31, 2005."[33] [emphasis supplied]

Fannie was able to make this statement because it defined subprime loans as loans it purchased from subprime lenders. Thus, in its 2007 10-K report, Fannie stated: "Subprime mortgage loans are typically originated by lenders specializing in these loans or by sub-prime divisions of large lenders, using processes unique to subprime loans. In reporting our subprime exposure, *we have classified mortgage loans as subprime if the mortgage loans are originated by one of these specialty lenders or a subprime division of a large lender.*"[34] [emphasis supplied] The credit scores on these loans, and the riskiness associated with those credit scores, were not deemed relevant. Accordingly, as late as its 2007 10-K report, Fannie was able to make the following statements, even though it is likely that, at that point, it held or guaranteed enough subprime loans to drive the company into insolvency if a substantial number of these loans were to default:

> Subprime mortgage loans, whether held in our portfolio or backing Fannie Mae MBS, represented *less than 1%* of our single-family business volume in each of 2007, 2006 and 2005.[35] [emphasis supplied]

---

31. Office of Comptroller of the Currency, Federal Reserve, Federal Deposit Insurance Corporation, and Office of Thrift Supervision advised in its "Expanded Guidance for Subprime Lending Programs," published in 2001, http://www.federalreserve.gov/Boarddocs/SRletters/2001/sr0104a1.pdf, that "the term 'subprime' refers to the credit characteristics of individual borrowers. Subprime borrowers typically have weakened credit histories that include payment delinquencies and possibly more severe problems such as charge-offs, judgments, and bankruptcies." A FICO score of 660 or below was evidence of "relatively high default probability."

32. Derived from table 12.

33. Fannie Mae, 2005 10-K report, filed May 2, 2007.

34. Fannie Mae, 2007 Form 10K, pp. 129 and 155.

35. Fannie Mae, 2007 Form 10K, p. 129.

We estimate that subprime mortgage loans held in our portfolio or subprime mortgage loans backing Fannie Mae MBS, excluding re-securitized private label mortgage related securities backed by subprime mortgage loans, represented approximately *0.3% of our single-family mortgage credit book of business* as of December 31, 2007, compared with 0.2% and 0.1% as of December 31, 2006 and 2005, respectively.[36] [emphasis supplied]

These statements could have lulled market participants and others—including the Lehman analysts—into believing that Fannie and Freddie did not hold or had not guaranteed substantial numbers of high-risk loans, and thus that there were many fewer such loans in the financial system than in fact existed.

Of course, in the early 2000s, there was no generally understood definition of the term "subprime," so Fannie and Freddie could define it as they liked, and the assumption that the GSEs only made prime loans continued to be supported by their public disclosures. So when Fannie and Freddie reported their loan acquisitions to various mortgage information aggregators, they did not report those mortgages as subprime or Alt-A, and the aggregators continued to follow industry practice by placing virtually all the GSEs' loans in the "prime" category. Without understanding Fannie and Freddie's peculiar and self-serving loan classification methods, the recipients of information about the GSEs' mortgage positions simply seemed to assume that all these mortgages were prime loans, as they had always been in the past, and added them to the number of prime loans outstanding. Accordingly, by 2008, there were approximately 12 million more NTMs in the financial system—and 12 million fewer prime loans—than most market participants realized.

Appendix 1 shows that the levels of delinquency and default would be 86 percent higher than expected if there were 12 million NTMs in the financial system instead of 12 million prime loans. Appendix 2 shows that the levels of delinquency would be 150 percent higher than expected if the feedback effect of mortgage delinquencies—causing lower housing prices, in a downward spiral—were taken into account. These differences in projected losses could have misled the rating agencies into believing that, even if the bubble were to deflate, the losses on mortgage failures would not be so substantial as to have a more than a local effect and would not adversely affect the AAA tranches in MBS securitizations.

The Commission never looked into this issue or attempted to determine the number of subprime and other NTMs that market participants believed to be outstanding in the system immediately before the financial crisis. Whenever possible in the Commission's public hearings, I asked analysts and other market participants how many NTMs they believed were outstanding before the financial crisis occurred. It was clear from the responses that none of the witnesses had ever considered that question, and it appeared that none suspected that the number was large enough to substantially affect losses after the collapse of the bubble.

It was only on November 10, 2008, after Fannie had been taken over by the federal government, that the company admitted in its 10-Q report for the third quarter of 2008 that it had classified as subprime or Alt-A loans only those loans that it purchased from

---

36. Fannie Mae, 2007 Form 10K, p. 130.

self-denominated subprime or Alt-A originators, and not loans that were subprime or Alt-A because of their risk characteristics. Even then Fannie wasn't fully candid. After describing its classification criteria, Fannie stated: "[H]owever, we have other loans with some features that are similar to Alt-A and subprime loans that we have not classified as Alt-A or subprime because they do not meet our classification criteria."[37] This hardly described the true nature of Fannie's obligations.

On the issue of the number of NTMs outstanding before the crisis, the Commission studiously averted its eyes, and the Commission majority's report never addresses the question. HUD's role in pressing for a reduction in mortgage underwriting standards escaped the FCIC's attention entirely, the GSEs' AH goals are mentioned only in passing, CRA is defended, and neither HUD's Best Practices Initiative nor FHA's activities is mentioned at all. No reason is advanced for the accumulation of subprime loans in the bubble other than the idea—implicit in the majority's report—that it was profitable. In sum, the majority's report is *Hamlet* without the prince of Denmark.

Indeed, the Commission's entire investigation seemed to be directed at minimizing the role of NTMs and the role of government housing policy. In the majority's telling, the NTMs were a "trigger" for the financial crisis, but once the collapse of the bubble had occurred, the "weaknesses and vulnerabilities" of the financial system—which had been there all along—caused the crisis. These alleged deficiencies included a lack of adequate regulation of the so-called "shadow banking system" and over-the-counter derivatives, the overly generous compensation arrangements on Wall Street, and securitization (characterized as "the originate to distribute model"). Coincidentally, all these purported weaknesses and vulnerabilities then required more government regulation, although their baleful presence hadn't been noted until an unprecedented number of subprime and Alt-A loans, created largely to comply with government housing policies, defaulted.

6. CONCLUSION

What is surprising about the many views of the causes of the financial crisis published since the Lehman bankruptcy, including the Commission's own inquiry, is the juxtaposition of two variables: (i) a general agreement that the bubble and the mortgage meltdown that followed its deflation were the precipitating causes—sometimes characterized as the "trigger"—of the financial crisis, and (ii) a seemingly studious effort to avoid examining how it came to be that mortgage underwriting standards declined to the point that the bubble contained so many NTMs that were ready to fail as soon as the bubble began to deflate. Instead of thinking through what would almost certainly happen when these assets

---

37. Fannie Mae, 2008 3rd quarter 10-Q, p. 115, http://www.fanniemae.com/ir/pdf/earnings/2008/q32008.pdf.

virtually disappeared from balance sheets, many observers—including the Commission majority in their report—pivoted immediately to blame the "weaknesses and vulnerabilities" of the free market or the financial or regulatory system, without considering whether *any* system could have survived such a blow.

One of the most striking examples of this approach was presented by Larry Summers, the head of the White House National Economic Council and one of President Obama's key advisers. In a private interview with a few of the members of the Commission (I was not informed of the interview), Summers was asked whether the mortgage meltdown was the cause of the financial crisis. His response was that the financial crisis was like a forest fire and the mortgage meltdown like a "cigarette butt" thrown into a very dry forest. Was the cigarette butt, he asked, the cause of the forest fire, or was it the tinder-dry condition of the forest?[38] The Commission majority adopted the idea that it was the tinder-dry forest. Their central argument is that the mortgage meltdown as the bubble deflated triggered the financial crisis because of the "vulnerabilities" inherent in the U.S. financial system at the time—the absence of regulation, lax regulation, predatory lending, greed on Wall Street, and, among participants in the securitization system, ineffective risk management and excessive leverage, among other factors. One of the majority's singular notions is that "thirty years of deregulation" had "stripped away key safeguards" against a crisis. This view ignores completely that in 1991, in the wake of the S&L crisis, Congress adopted the FDIC Improvement Act, which was by far the toughest bank regulatory law since the advent of deposit insurance and was celebrated at the time of its enactment as finally giving the regulators the power to put an end to bank crises.

The forest metaphor turns out to be an excellent way to communicate the difference between the Commission majority's report and this dissenting statement. What Summers characterized as a "cigarette butt" was 27 million high-risk NTMs with a total value over $4.5 trillion. Let's use a little common sense here: $4.5 trillion in high-risk loans was *not* a "cigarette butt;" it was more like an exploding gasoline truck in that forest. The Commission majority's report blames the conditions in the financial system; I blame 27 million subprime and Alt-A mortgages—half of all mortgages outstanding in the U.S. in 2008—a number that appears to have been unknown to most, if not all, market participants at the time. No financial system, in my view, could have survived the failure of such large numbers of high-risk mortgages once the bubble began to deflate, and no market could have avoided a panic when it became clear that the number of defaults and delinquencies among these mortgages far exceeded anything that even the most sophisticated market participants expected.

This conclusion has significant policy implications. If, in fact, the financial crisis was caused by government housing policies, then the Dodd-Frank Act was legislative overreach and unnecessary. The appropriate policy choice was to reduce or eliminate the government's involvement in the residential mortgage markets, not to impose significant new regulation on the financial system.

---

38. FCIC, Summers interview, p. 77.

The balance of this statement will outline (i) how the high levels of delinquency and default among the NTMs were transmitted as losses to the financial system, and (ii) how the government policies summarized above caused the accumulation of an unprecedented number of NTMs in the United States and around the globe.

PART II

How 27 Million NTMs Precipitated a Financial Crisis

Although the Commission never defined the financial crisis it was supposed to investigate, it is necessary to have a definition in order to know where to start and stop. If, for example, the financial crisis is still continuing, then the effect of government policies such as the Troubled Asset Repurchase Program (TARP) should be evaluated.

However, it seems clear that Congress wanted the Commission to concentrate on what caused the unprecedented events that occurred largely in the fall of 2008, and for this purpose, Ben Bernanke's definition of the financial crisis seems most appropriate:

> The credit boom began to unravel in early 2007 when problems surfaced with sub-prime mortgages—mortgages offered to less-creditworthy borrowers—and house prices in parts of the country began to fall. Mortgage delinquencies and defaults rose, and the downturn in house prices intensified, trends that continue today. Investors, stunned by losses on assets they had believed to be safe, began to pull back from a wide range of credit markets, and financial institutions—reeling from severe losses on mortgages and other loans—cut back their lending. The crisis deepened [in September 2008], when the failure or near-failure of several major financial firms caused many financial and credit markets to freeze up.[1]

In other words, the financial crisis was the result of the losses suffered by financial institutions around the world when U.S. mortgages began to fail in large numbers. The crisis became more severe in September 2008, when the failure of several major financial

---

1. Speech at Morehouse College, April 14, 2009.

firms—which held or were thought to hold large amounts of mortgage-related assets—caused many financial markets to freeze up. This summary encapsulates a large number of interconnected events, but it makes clear that the underlying cause of the financial crisis was a rapid decline in the value of one specific and widely held asset: U.S. residential mortgages. The next question is how, exactly, these delinquencies and losses caused the financial crisis.

The following discussion will show that it was not all mortgages and mortgage-backed securities that were the source of the crisis, but NTMs in particular—including PMBS backed by NTMs. Traditional mortgages, which were generally prime mortgages, did not suffer substantial losses at the outset of the mortgage meltdown, although as the financial crisis turned into a recession and housing prices continued to fall, losses among prime mortgages began to approach the level of prime mortgage losses that had occurred in past housing crises. However, those levels were far lower than the losses on NTMs, which reached levels of delinquency and default between 15 and 45 percent (depending on the characteristics of the loans in question) because the loans involved were weaker as a class than in any previous housing crisis. The fact that they were also far larger in number than in any previous bubble was what caused the catastrophic housing price declines that fueled the financial crisis.

1. How Failures among NTMs Were Transmitted to the Financial System

When the housing bubble began to deflate in mid-2007, delinquency rates among NTMs began to increase substantially. Previously, although these mortgages were weak and high-risk, their delinquency rates were relatively low. This was a consequence of the bubble itself, which inflated housing prices so that homes could be sold with no loss in cases where borrowers could not meet their mortgage obligations. Alternatively, rising housing prices—coupled with liberal appraisal rules—created a form of free equity in a home, allowing the home to be refinanced easily, perhaps even at a lower interest rate. However, rising housing prices eventually reached the point where even easy credit terms could no longer keep the good times rolling, and at that point the bubble flattened and weak mortgages became exposed for what they were. As Warren Buffett has said, when the tide goes out, you can see who's swimming naked.

The role of the government's housing policy is crucial at this point. As discussed earlier, if the government had not been directing money into the mortgage markets in order to foster growth in home ownership, NTMs in the bubble would have begun to default relatively soon after they were originated. The continuous inflow of government or government-backed funds, however, kept the bubble growing—not only in size but over time—and this tended to suppress the significant delinquencies and defaults that had brought previous bubbles to an end in only three or four years. That explains why PMBS based on NTMs could become so numerous and so risky without triggering the delinquencies and defaults that caused earlier bubbles to deflate within a shorter period. With few losses and time to continue originations, Countrywide and others were able to securitize subprime PMBS in increasingly large amounts from 2002 ($134 billion) to 2006 ($483 billion) without engendering the substantial increase in delinquencies that ordinarily would have alarmed investors and brought the bubble to a halt.[2]

Indeed, the absence of delinquencies had the opposite effect. As investors around the world saw housing prices rise in the United States without any significant losses even among subprime and other high-yielding loans, they were encouraged to buy PMBS that—although rated AAA—still offered attractive yields. In other words, as shown in figure 2, government housing policies—AH goals imposed on the GSEs, the decline in FHA lending standards, HUD's pressure for reduced underwriting standards among mortgage bankers, and CRA requirements for insured banks—increased the worldwide demand for subprime PMBS by encouraging the growth of the bubble. Then, in mid-2007, the bubble began to deflate, with catastrophic consequences.

2. THE DEFAULTS BEGIN

The best summary of how the deflation of the housing bubble led to the financial crisis was contained in the prepared testimony that FDIC chair Sheila Bair delivered to the FCIC in a September 2 hearing:

> Starting in mid-2007, global financial markets began to experience serious *liquidity challenges* related mainly to rising concerns about U.S. mortgage credit quality. As *home prices fell*, recently originated subprime and *non-traditional mortgage loans began to default at record rates*. These developments led to *growing concerns* about the value of financial positions in mortgage-backed securities and related derivative instruments held by major financial institutions in the U.S. and around the world. The *difficulty in determining the value* of mortgage-related assets and, therefore, the *balance-sheet strength* of large banks and non-bank financial institutions ultimately led these institutions to become *wary of lending* to one another, even on a short-term basis.[3] [emphasis supplied]

All the important elements of what happened are in Chairman Bair's succinct statement: (i) in mid-2007, the markets began to experience liquidity challenges because of concerns about the credit quality of NTMs; (ii) housing prices fell and NTMs began to default at record rates; (iii) it was difficult to determine the value of MBS, and thus the financial condition of the institutions that held them; and (iv) finally, as a consequence of this

2. Inside Mortgage Finance, *The 2009 Mortgage Market Statistical Annual—Volume II,* MBS database.

3. Sheila C. Bair, "Systemically Important Institutions and the Issue of 'Too-Big-to-Fail,'" Testimony to the FCIC, September 2, 2010, p. 3.

uncertainty—especially after the failure of Lehman—financial institutions would not lend to one another. That phenomenon *was* the financial crisis. The following discussion will show how each of these steps operated to bring down the financial system.

Markets Began to Experience Liquidity Challenges

To understand the transmission mechanism, it is necessary to distinguish between PMBS, on the one hand, and the MBS that were distributed by government agencies such as FHA/ Ginnie Mae, and the GSEs (referred to jointly as "Agencies" in this section). As shown in table 1, by 2008, the 27 million NTMs in the U.S. financial system in 2008 were held as (i) whole mortgages, (ii) MBS guaranteed by the GSEs or insured or held by a government agency or a bank under the CRA, or (iii) as PMBS securitized by private firms such as Countrywide. The 27 million NTMs had an aggregate unpaid principal balance of more than $4.5 trillion, and the portion represented by PMBS consisted of 7.8 million mortgages with an aggregate unpaid principal balance of approximately $1.9 trillion. As mortgage delinquencies and defaults multiplied in the U.S. financial system, the losses were transmitted to financial institutions through their holdings of PMBS. How did this happen, and what role was played by government housing policy?

Both Agency MBS and PMBS pass through to investors the principal and interest received on the mortgages in a pool that backs an issue of securities; the difference between them is the way they protect investors against credit risk—i.e., the possibility of losses in the event that the mortgages in the pool begin to default. The Agencies insure or place a guarantee on all the securities issued by a pool they or some other entity create. Because of the Agencies' real or perceived government backing, all of these securities are rated or considered to be AAA.

PMBS rely on a classification and subordination system known as "tranching" to provide some investors in the pool with a degree of assurance that they will not suffer losses because of mortgage defaults. In the tranching system, different classes of securities are issued by the pool. The rights of some classes to receive payments of principal and interest from the mortgages in the pool are subordinated to the rights of other classes, so that the superior classes are more likely to receive payment even if there are some defaults among the mortgages in the pool.

Through this mechanism, approximately 90 percent of an issue of PMBS could be rated AAA or AA, even if the underlying mortgages are NTMs that have a higher rate of delinquency than prime loans. In theory, for example, if the historic rates of loss on a pool of NTMs is, say, five percent, then those losses will be absorbed by the 10 percent of the securities holders who are in the classes rated lower than AAA or AA. Of course, if the losses are greater than anticipated—exactly what happened as the recent bubble began to deflate—they will reach into the higher classes and substantially reduce their value.[4] It

---

4. A thorough description of the tranching system, and many more details about various methods of protecting senior tranches, is contained in Gary B. Gorton, *Slapped By the Invisible Hand: The Panic of 2007*, Oxford University Press, 2010, pp. 82–113.

is not clear whether, in 2007 or 2008, mortgage delinquencies and defaults had actually caused cash losses in the AAA tranches of PMBS, but the rate at which delinquencies and defaults among NTMs were occurring throughout the financial system was so high that such losses were a distinct possibility—obviously a matter of great concern to investors.

This means that investors in PMBS and government-backed Agency MBS had different experiences when the bubble began to deflate. Those who invested in Agency MBS did not suffer losses (the U.S. government has thus far protected all investors in Agency MBS), while those who invested in PMBS were exposed to losses if the losses on the underlying mortgages were so great that they threatened to invade the AAA and AA classes. Even if no cash losses had actually been suffered, the holders of PMBS would see a sharp decline in the market value of their holdings as investors, shocked by the large number of defaults on mortgages, fled the asset-backed market. So when we look for the *direct* effect of mortgage failures on the financial condition of various financial institutions in the financial crisis, we should look only to the PMBS, not the MBS issued by the Agencies.

In addition, the default and delinquency ratios on the loans underlying the PMBS were higher than similar ratios among the loans held or guaranteed by the Agencies. Many of the loans that backed the PMBS were the self-denominated subprime loans (that is, made by subprime lenders explicitly to subprime borrowers) and were classified in the worst-performing categories in table 3. In part, the better-performing characteristics of the NTMs held or guaranteed by the Agencies were due to the fact that the Agencies were not buying for economic purposes—to make profits—but only to meet government requirements, such as the AH goals. They did not want or need the higher-yielding and thus more risky mortgages that backed the PMBS, because they did not need higher yields in order to sell their MBS. In addition, because of their lower-cost funding, the Agencies could pay more for the NTMs they bought and thus could acquire the "best of the worst."

PMBS Are Connected to All Other NTMs through Housing Prices

But this does not mean that only the failure of the PMBS was responsible for the financial crisis. In a sense, all mortgages are linked to one another through housing prices, and housing prices, in turn, are highly sensitive to delinquencies and defaults on mortgages. This is a characteristic of mortgages that is not present in other securitized assets. If a credit card holder defaults on his obligations, it has little effect on other credit card holders, but if a homeowner defaults on a mortgage, the resulting foreclosure has an effect on the value of all homes in the vicinity and thus on the quality of all mortgages on those homes.

Accordingly, the PMBS were intimately connected—through housing prices—to the NTMs securitized by the Agencies. Because there were so many more NTMs held or securitized by the Agencies (see table 1), their unprecedented numbers—even in cases where they had a lower average rate of delinquency and default than the NTMs that backed the PMBS—was the major source of downward pressure on housing prices throughout the United States. Weakening housing prices, in turn, caused more mortgage defaults, among both NTMs in general and the particular NTMs that were the collateral for PMBS. In other words, the NTMs underlying the PMBS were weakened by the delinquencies and defaults among the much larger number of mortgages held or guaranteed as MBS by the Agencies.

In reality, then, the losses on the PMBS were much higher than they would have been if the government's housing policies had not brought into being 19 million other NTMs that were failing in unprecedented numbers. These failures drove down housing prices by 30 percent—an unprecedented decline—which multiplied the losses on the PMBS.

Finally, the funds that the government directed into the housing market in pursuit of its social policies enlarged the housing bubble and extended it in time. The longer housing bubbles grow, the riskier the mortgages they contain; lenders are constantly trying to find ways to keep monthly mortgage payments down while borrowers are buying more expensive houses. While the bubble was growing, the risks that were building within it were obscured. Borrowers who would otherwise have defaulted on their loans, bringing an end to the bubble, were able to use the rising home prices to refinance, sometimes at lower interest rates. With delinquency rates relatively low, investors did not have a reason to exit the mortgage markets, and the continuing flow of funds into mortgages allowed the bubble to extend for an unprecedented ten years. This, in turn, enabled the PMBS market to grow to enormous size and thus to have a more calamitous effect when it finally collapsed. If the government policies that provided a continuing source of funding for the bubble had not been pursued, it is doubtful that there would have been a PMBS market remotely as large as the one that developed, or that—when the housing bubble collapsed—the losses to financial institutions would have been as great.

PMBS, as Securities, Are Vulnerable to Investor Sentiment

In addition to their link to the Agencies' NTMs through housing prices, PMBS were particularly vulnerable to changes in investor sentiment about mortgages. The fact that the mortgages underlying the PMBS were held in securitized form was an important element of the crisis. There are many reasons for the popularity of mortgage securitization. Beginning in 2002, for example, the Basel regulations provided that mortgages held in the form of MBS—presumably because of their superior liquidity compared to whole mortgages—required a bank to hold only 1.6 percent risk-based capital, while whole mortgages required risk-based capital backing of 4 percent. This made all forms of MBS, including PMBS, much less expensive to hold than whole mortgages. In addition, mortgages in securitized form could be traded more easily and used more readily as a source of liquidity through repurchase agreements.

However, some of the benefits of securitized mortgages are also detriments when certain mortgage market conditions prevail. If housing values are declining, losses on whole mortgages are recognized only slowly in bank financial statements and will be recognized even more slowly in the larger market. PMBS, however, are far more vulnerable to swings in sentiment than whole mortgages held on bank balance sheets. First, because they are more easily traded, PMBS values can be more quickly and adversely affected by negative information about the underlying mortgages than whole mortgages in the same principal amount. PMBS markets tend to be thin because PMBS pools differ from one another. If investors believe that mortgages in general are declining in value, or if they learn of a substantial and

FIGURE 3
THE MBS MARKET REACTS TO THE BUBBLE'S DEFLATION

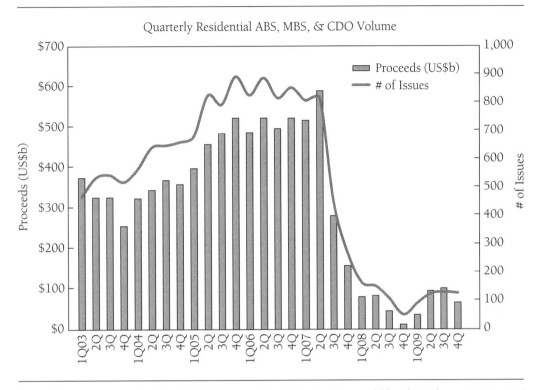

Quarterly Residential ABS, MBS, & CDO Volume

SOURCES: Thompson Reuters *Debt Capital Markets Review,* Fourth Quarter 2008, available at http://thomsonreuters.com/ products_services/financial/league_tables/debt_equity/ (accessed July 30, 2009)

unexpected number of defaults and delinquencies, they may abandon the market for all PMBS, causing the general PMBS price level to fall precipitously.

For example, in his book *Slapped by the Invisible Hand,* Professor Gary Gorton of Yale notes that the ABX index, initially published in late 2006, gave investors for the first time a picture of how others saw the value of a selected group of PMBS pools. The index showed steeply declining values, which caused many investors to withdraw from the market. Gorton observed: "I view the ABX indices as revealing hitherto unknown information, namely, the aggregated view that subprime was worth significantly less. . . It is not clear whether the housing bubble was burst by the ability to short the subprime housing market or whether house prices were going down and the implications of this were aggregated and revealed by the ABX indices."[5]

Whatever the underlying reason, as shown in figure 3, this seems to be exactly what happened in the financial crisis. The result was a crash in the MBS market as investors fled what looked like major oncoming losses.

The decline in housing values had a profound adverse effect on the liquidity of all financial institutions that were exposed to PMBS. As noted above, one of the benefits of holding PMBS, especially those with AAA ratings, was that they were readily marketable. As such,

---

5. Gorton, *Slapped by the Invisible Hand,* note 41, pp. 121–23.

they were considered sound and secure investments, carried on balance sheets at par and suitable to serve as collateral for short-term financing through repurchase agreements, or repos. In a repo transaction, a borrower sells a security to a lender with an option to repurchase it at a price that provides the lender with a return appropriate for a secured loan. The lender assumes that if its counterparty defaults, the collateral can be sold. Accordingly, if the collateral asset loses its reputation for high quality and liquidity, it loses much of its value for both capital and liquidity purposes, even if the collateral itself has not actually suffered losses. This is what happened to AAA-rated PMBS as housing prices first leveled off and then began to fall in 2007, and as mortgage delinquencies rolled in at rates no one had expected. As discussed more fully below, when AAA-rated PMBS became unmarketable, they lost their value for liquidity purposes, making it difficult or impossible for many financial institutions to fund themselves using these assets as collateral for repos. This was the "liquidity challenge" to which Chairman Bair referred in her testimony.

The near-failure of Bear Stearns in March 2008 was an excellent example of how the unexpected collapse of the PMBS market could cause a substantial loss of liquidity by a financial institution, and ultimately its inability to survive the resulting loss in market confidence. The FCIC staff's review of the liquidity problems of Bear Stearns showed that the loss of the PMBS market was the single event that was crippling for Bear, because it eliminated a major portion of the firm's liquidity pool—AAA-rated PMBS—as a useful source of repo financing. According to the Commission staff's Preliminary Investigative Report on Bear, prepared for hearings on May 5 and 6, 2010, 97.4 percent of Bear's short-term funding was secured and only 2.6 percent unsecured. "As of January 11, 2008," the FCIC staff reported, "$45.9 billion of Bear Stearns' repo collateral was composed of agency (Fannie and Freddie) mortgage-related securities, $23.7 billion was in non-agency securitized asset backed securities [i.e., PMBS], and $19 billion was in whole loans."[6] The Agency MBS were unaffected by the collapse of the PMBS market and could still be used for funding.

Thus, about 27 percent of Bear's readily available sources of funding consisted of PMBS that became unusable for repo financing when the PMBS market disappeared. The loss of this source of liquidity put the firm in serious jeopardy; rumors swept the market about Bear's condition, and clients began withdrawing funds. Bear's officers told the Commission that the firm was profitable in its first 2008 quarter—the quarter in which it failed; ironically, they also told the Commission's staff that they had moved Bear's short-term funding from commercial paper to MBS because they believed that collateral-backed funding would be more stable. In the week beginning March 10, 2008, according to the FCIC staff report, Bear had over $18 billion in cash reserves, but by March 13, the liquidity pool had fallen to $2 billion.[7] It was clear that Bear—solvent and profitable or not—could not survive a run that was fueled by fear and uncertainty about its liquidity and the possibility of its insolvency.

Parenthetically, it should be noted that the Commission's staff focused on Bear because the Commission's majority apparently believed that the business model of investment

---

6. FCIC, "Investigative Findings on Bear Stearns (Preliminary Draft)," April 29, 2010, p. 16.
7. Id., p. 45.

banks, which relied on relatively high leverage and repo or other short-term financing, was inherently unstable. The need to rescue Bear was thought to be evidence of this fact. Clearly, the five independent investment banks—Bear, Lehman Brothers, Merrill Lynch, Morgan Stanley and Goldman Sachs—were badly damaged in the financial crisis. Only two of them remain independent firms, and those two are now regulated as bank holding companies by the Federal Reserve. Nevertheless, it is not clear that the investment banks fared any worse than the much more heavily regulated commercial banks—or Fannie and Freddie, which were also regulated more stringently than the investment banks but not as stringently as banks. The investment banks did not pass the test created by the mortgage meltdown and the subsequent financial crisis, but neither did a large number of insured banks—IndyMac, Washington Mutual (WaMu) and Wachovia, to name the largest—that were much more heavily regulated and, in addition, offered insured deposits and had access to the Fed's discount window if they needed emergency funds to deal with runs. The view of the Commission majority, that investment banks—as part of the so-called "shadow banking system"—were special contributors to the financial crisis, seems misplaced for this reason. They are better classified not as contributors to the financial crisis but as victims of the panic that ensued after the housing bubble and the PMBS market collapsed.

Bear went down because the delinquencies and failures of an unprecedentedly large number of NTMs caused the collapse of the PMBS market; this destroyed the usefulness of AAA-rated PMBS that Bear and others relied on as assets for both capital and liquidity, and thus raised questions about the firm's ability to meet its obligations. Investment banks like Bear Stearns were not commercial banks; instead of using short-term deposits to hold long-term assets—the hallmark of a bank—their business model relied on short-term funding to carry the short-term assets of a trading business. Contrary to the views of the Commission majority, there is nothing inherently wrong with that business model, but it could not survive an unprecedented financial panic as severe as that which followed the collapse in value of an asset class as large and as liquid as AAA-rated subprime PMBS.

Mortgage Defaults at Record Rates Created Balance Sheet Losses

Chairman Bair also pointed to the relationship between the decline in the value of PMBS and "the *balance sheet strength*" of the financial institutions that held these assets. Adding to liquidity-based losses, balance sheet writedowns were another major element of the loss transmission mechanism. Securitized assets held by financial institutions are subject to the rules of fair value accounting and must be marked to market under certain circumstances. Thus, banks and other financial institutions that are holding securitized mortgages in the form of PMBS could be subject to large *accounting* losses—but not necessarily cash losses—if investor sentiment were to turn against securitized mortgages and market values were to decline. Accordingly, once large numbers of delinquencies and losses started showing up in the mortgage markets generally and in the mortgage pools that backed the PMBS, it was *not necessary* for all the losses to be realized before the PMBS lost substantial value. All that was necessary was that the market for these assets became seriously impaired. This is exactly what happened in the middle of 2007, leading immediately not only to severe adverse liquidity consequences for financial institutions that held PMBS but also to capital writedowns that made them appear unstable and possibly insolvent.

These mark-to-market capital losses could be greater than the actual credit losses to be anticipated. As one Federal Reserve study put it: "The financial turmoil . . . put downward pressure on prices of structured finance products across the whole spectrum of [asset-backed] securities, even those with only minimal ties to the riskiest underlying assets . . . [I]n addition to discounts from higher expected credit risk, large mark-to-market discounts are generated by uncertainty about the quality of the underlying assets, by illiquidity, and by price volatility . . . This illiquidity discount is the main reason why the mark-to-market discount here, and in most similar analyses, is larger than the expected credit default rates on underlying assets."[8] In other words, the illiquidity discount associated with the uncertainties in value of collateral can be substantially larger than the credit default spread, since the spread reflects only anticipated credit losses.

As shown so dramatically in figure 3, the collapse of the market for PMBS was a seminal event in the history of the financial crisis. Even though delinquencies had only just begun to show up in mortgage pools, the absence of a functioning market meant that PMBS simply could not be sold at anything but distress prices. The inability of financial institutions to liquidate their PMBS assets at anything like earlier values had dire consequences, especially under mark-to-market accounting rules, and was the crux of the crisis. In effect, a whole class of assets—involving almost $2 trillion—came to be called "toxic assets" in the media and had to be written down substantially on the balance sheets of financial institutions around the world. Although this made financial institutions look weaker than they actually were, the PMBS they held, despite being unmarketable at that point, were in many cases still flowing cash at close-to-expected rates. Instead of a slow decline in value—which would have occurred if whole mortgages were held on bank balance sheets and gradually deteriorated in quality—the loss of marketability of these securities caused a crash in value.

The Commission majority did not discuss the significance of mark-to-market accounting in its report. This was a serious lapse, given the views of many that accounting policies played an important role in the financial crisis. Many commentators have argued that the resulting impairment charges to balance sheets reduced the Generally Accepted Accounting Principles (GAAP) equity of financial institutions and, therefore, their capital positions, making them appear financially weaker than they actually were if viewed on the basis of the cash flows they were receiving.[9]

The investor panic that began when unanticipated and unprecedented losses started to appear among NTMs generally and in the PMBS mortgage pools now spread to financial institutions themselves; investors were no longer sure which of these institutions could survive severe mortgage-related losses. This process was succinctly described in an analysis

---

8. Daniel Beltran, Laurie Pounder, and Charles Thomas, "Foreign Exposure to Asset-Backed Securities of U.S. Origin," Board of Governors of the Federal Reserve System, *International Finance Discussion Papers* 939, August 2008, pp. 11–14.

9. FCIC Draft Staff Report, "The Role of Accounting During the Financial Crisis," p. 16.

of fair value or mark-to-market accounting in the financial crisis issued by the Institute of International Finance, an organization of the world's largest banks and financial firms:

> [O]ften-dramatic write-downs of *sound* assets required under the current implementation of fair-value accounting adversely affect market sentiment, in turn leading to further write-downs, margin calls and capital impacts in a downward spiral that may lead to large-scale fire-sales of assets, and destabilizing, pro-cyclical feedback effects. These damaging feedback effects worsen liquidity problems and contribute to the conversion of liquidity problems into solvency problems.[10] [emphasis in the original]

At least one study attempted to assess the effect of this on financial institutions overall. In January 2009, Nouriel Roubini and Elisa Parisi-Capone estimated the mark-to-market losses on MBS backed by both prime loans and NTMs. Their estimate was slightly over $1 trillion, of which U.S. banks and investment banks were estimated to have lost $318 billion on a mark-to-market basis.[11]

This would be a dramatic loss if all of it were realized. In 2008, the U.S. banking system had total assets of $10 trillion; the five largest investment banks had total assets of $4 trillion.[12] If we assume that the banks had a leverage ratio of about 15-to-1 in 2008, and the investment banks about 30-to-1, that would mean that the equity capital position of the banking industry as a whole would be about $650 billion, and the same number for the investment banks would be about $130 billion, for a total of $780 billion. Under these circumstances, the collapse of the PMBS market alone reduced the capital positions of U.S. banks and investment banks by approximately 41 percent on a mark-to-market basis. This does not mean that any actual losses were suffered, only that the assets concerned might have to be written down or could not be sold for the price at which they were previously carried on the firm's balance sheet.

In addition, Roubini and Parisi-Capone estimated that U.S. commercial and investment banks suffered a further mark-to-market loss of $225 billion on unsecuritized subprime and Alt-A mortgages.[13] They also estimated that mark-to-market losses for financial institutions outside the United States would be about 40 percent of U.S. losses, so there was likely to be a major effect on banks and other financial institutions around the world—depending, of course, on their capital position at the time the PMBS market stopped functioning. I am not aware of any data showing the mark-to-market effect of the collapse of the PMBS market on other U.S. financial institutions, but it can be assumed that they also suffered similar losses in proportion to their holdings of PMBS.

10. Institute of International Finance, "IIF Board of Directors—Discussion Memorandum on Valuation in Illiquid Markets," April 7, 2008, p. 1.

11. Nouriel Roubini and Elisa Parisi-Carbone, "Total $3.6 Trillion Projected Loan and Securities Losses in U.S. $1.8 Trillion of Which Borne by U.S. Banks/Brokers," *RGE Monitor,* January 2009, p. 8.

12. Timothy F. Geithner, "Reducing Systemic Risk in a Dynamic Financial System," Remarks at the Economic Club of New York, June 9, 2008, available at http://www.ny.frb.org/newsevents/speeches/2008/tfg080609.html.

13. Roubini and Parisi-Carbone, "Total $3.6 Trillion Projected Loan and Securities Losses," p. 7.

Losses of this magnitude would certainly be enough—when combined with other losses on securities and loans not related to mortgages—to call into question the stability of a large number of banks, investment banks and other financial institutions in the United States and around the world. However, there was one other factor that exacerbated the adverse effect of the loss of a market for PMBS. Although accounting rules did not require all PMBS to be written down, investors and counterparties did not know which financial institutions were holding the weakest assets and how much of their assets would have to be written down over time. Whatever that amount, it would reduce their capital positions at a time when investors and counterparties were anxious about their stability. This was the "balance sheet effect" that was the third element of Chairman Bair's summary.

To summarize, then, the following are the steps through which the government's housing policies transmitted losses—through PMBS—to the largest financial institutions: (i) the 19 million NTMs acquired or guaranteed by the Agencies were major contributors to the growth of the bubble and its extension in time; (ii) the growth of the bubble suppressed the losses that would ordinarily have brought the development of NTM-backed PMBS to a halt; (iii) competition for NTMs drove subprime lenders further out on the risk curve to find high-yielding mortgages to securitize, especially when these loans did not appear to be producing losses commensurate with their risk; (iv) when the bubble finally burst, the unprecedented number of delinquencies and defaults among all NTMs—the great majority of which were held or guaranteed by the Agencies—caused investors to flee the PMBS market, reducing the liquidity of the financial institutions that held the PMBS; and (v) mark-to-market accounting required these institutions to write down the value of the PMBS they held, as well as their other mortgage-related assets, reducing their capital positions and raising further questions about their stability and solvency.

Government Actions Create a Panic

More than any other phenomenon, the financial crisis of 2008 resembles an old-fashioned investor and creditor panic. In the classic study *Manias, Panics and Crashes: A History of Financial Crises,* Charles Kindleberger and Robert Aliber make a distinction between a remote cause and a proximate cause of a panic: "*Causa remota* of any crisis is the expansion of credit and speculation, while *causa proxima* is some incident that saps the confidence of the system and induces investors to sell commodities, stocks, real estate, bills of exchange, or promissory notes and increase their money holdings."[14] In the great financial panic of 2008, it is reasonably clear that the remote cause was the buildup of NTMs in the financial system, primarily—as I have shown in this analysis—as a result of government housing policy. This unprecedented increase in weak and risky assets set the financial system up for a crisis of some kind. The event that turned a potential crisis into a full-fledged panic—the proximate cause of the panic—was also the government's action: the rescue of Bear Stearns in March 2008 and the subsequent failure to rescue Lehman Brothers six months later. In

---

14. Charles P. Kindleberger and Robert Aliber, *Manias, Panics, and Crashes: A History of Financial Crises,* 5th edition, John Wiley & Sons, Inc., 2005, p. 104.

terms of its ultimate cost to the public, this was one of the great policy errors of all time, and the reasons for the misjudgments that led to it have not yet been fully explored.

The lesson taught by the rescue of Bear was that all large financial institutions—and especially those larger than Bear—would be rescued by the government. The moral hazard introduced by this one act irreparably changed the position of Lehman Brothers and every other large firm in the world's financial system. From that time forward, (i) the critical need for more capital became less critical; the likelihood of a government bailout would reassure creditors, so there was no need to dilute the shareholders any further by raising additional capital; (ii) firms such as Lehman that might have been saved through an acquisition by a larger firm or an infusion of fresh capital by a strategic investor drove harder bargains with potential acquirers; (iii) the potential acquirers themselves waited for the U.S. government to pick up some of the cost, as it had with Bear—an offer that never came in Lehman's case; and (iv) the Reserve Fund, a money market mutual fund, apparently assuming that Lehman would be rescued, decided not to sell the heavily discounted Lehman commercial paper it held; instead, with devastating results for the money market fund industry, it waited to be bailed out.

But Lehman was not saved, and its creditors were not bailed out. At a time when large mark-to-market losses among U.S. financial firms raised questions about which large financial institutions were insolvent or unstable, the demise of Lehman was a major shock. It overturned all the rational expectations about government policies that market participants had developed after the Bear rescue. With no certainty about who was strong or who was weak, there was a headlong rush to U.S. government securities. Banks—afraid that their counterparties would want a return of their investments or their corporate customers would draw on lines of credit—began to hoard cash. Banks wouldn't lend to other banks, even overnight. As Chairman Bair suggested, that *was* the financial crisis. Everything after that was simply cleaning up the mess.

This analysis lays the principal cause of the financial crisis squarely at the feet of the unprecedented number of NTMs that were brought into the U.S. financial markets by government housing policy. These weak and high-risk loans helped to build the bubble, and when the bubble deflated, they defaulted in unprecedented numbers. This threatened losses in the PMBS that were held by financial institutions in the United States and around the world, impairing both their liquidity and their apparent stability.

The accumulation of 27 million subprime and Alt-A mortgages was not a random event, or even the result of major forces such as global financial imbalances or excessively low interest rates. Instead, these loans and the bubble to which they contributed were the direct consequence of something far more mundane: U.S. government housing policy, which—led by HUD over two administrations—deliberately reduced mortgage underwriting standards so that more people could buy homes. While this process was going on, everyone was pleased. Homeownership in the United States actually grew to the highest level ever recorded. But the result was a financial catastrophe from which the United States has still not recovered.

PART III

The U.S. Government's Role in Fostering the Growth of the NTM Market

The preceding section of this dissenting statement described the damage that was done to the financial system by the unprecedented number of defaults and delinquencies that occurred among the 27 million NTMs that were present in 2008. Given the damage they caused, the most important question about the financial crisis is why so many low-quality mortgages were created. Another way to state this question is to ask why mortgage standards declined so substantially before and during the 1997–2007 bubble, allowing so many NTMs to be created. This massive and unprecedented change in underwriting standards had to have a cause—some factor that was present during the 1990s and thereafter that was not present in any earlier period. Part III addresses this fundamental question.

The conventional explanation for the financial crisis is the one given by Fed Chairman Bernanke in the same speech at Morehouse College quoted at the outset of Part II:

> Saving inflows from abroad can be beneficial if the country that receives those inflows invests them well. Unfortunately, that was not always the case in the United States and some other countries. *Financial institutions reacted to the surplus of available funds by competing aggressively for borrowers, and, in the years leading up to the crisis, credit to both households and businesses became relatively cheap and easy to obtain.* One important consequence was a housing boom in the United States, a boom that was fueled in large part by a rapid expansion of mortgage lending. *Unfortunately, much of this lending was poorly done, involving, for example, little or no down payment by the borrower or insufficient consideration by the lender of the borrower's ability to make the monthly payments.* Lenders may have become careless because they, like many people at the time, expected that house prices would continue to rise—thereby allowing borrowers to build up equity in their homes—and

that credit would remain easily available, so that borrowers would be able to refinance if necessary. *Regulators did not do enough to prevent poor lending, in part because many of the worst loans were made by firms subject to little or no federal regulation.*[1] [emphasis supplied]

In other words, the liquidity in the world financial market caused U.S. banks to compete for borrowers by lowering their underwriting standards for mortgages and other loans. Lenders became careless. Regulators failed. Unregulated originators made bad loans. One has to ask: is it plausible that banks would compete for borrowers by lowering their mortgage standards? Mortgage originators—whether S&Ls, commercial banks, mortgage banks, or unregulated brokers—have been competing for one hundred years. That competition involved offering the lowest rates and the most benefits to potential borrowers. It did not, however, generally result in or involve the weakening of underwriting standards. Those standards—what made up the traditional U.S. mortgage—were generally fifteen- or thirty-year amortizing loans to homebuyers who could provide a downpayment of at least 10 to 20 percent and had good credit records, jobs, and steady incomes. Because of its inherent quality, this loan was known as a "prime mortgage."

There were subprime loans and subprime lenders, but in the early 1990s, subprime lenders were generally niche players that made loans to people who could not get traditional mortgage loans; the number of loans they generated was relatively small and bore higher-than-normal interest rates to compensate for the risks of default. In addition, mortgage bankers and others relied on FHA insurance for loans with low downpayments, impaired credit, and high debt ratios. Until the 1990s, these NTMs were never more than a fraction of the total number of mortgages outstanding. The reason that low underwriting standards were not generally used is simple. Low standards would result in large losses when these mortgages defaulted, and very few lenders wanted to hold such mortgages. In addition, Fannie and Freddie were the buyers for most middle-class mortgages in the United States, and they were conservative in their approach. Unless an originator made a traditional mortgage, it was unlikely that Fannie or Freddie or another secondary market buyer could be found for it.

This is common sense. If you produce an inferior product—whether it's a household cleaner, an automobile, or a loan—people soon recognize the lack of quality and you are out of business. This was not the experience with mortgages, which became weaker and riskier as the 1990s and 2000s progressed. Why did this happen?

In its report, the Commission majority seemed to assume that originators of mortgages controlled the quality of mortgages. Much is made in the majority's report of the so-called "originate to distribute" idea, where an originator is not supposed to care about the quality of the mortgages because they would eventually be sold off. The originator, it is said, has no "skin in the game." The motivation for making poor-quality mortgages in this telling is to earn fees, not only on the origination but in each of the subsequent steps in the securitization process.

This theory turns the mortgage market upside down. Mortgage originators could make all the low-quality mortgages they wanted, but they wouldn't earn a dime unless there was a *buyer*. The real question, then, is why there were buyers for inferior mortgages and this, as it

---

1. Speech at Morehead College, April 14, 2009.

turns out, is the same as asking why mortgage underwriting standards, beginning in the early 1990s, deteriorated so badly. As Professor Raghuram Rajan notes in *Fault Lines:* "[A]s brokers came to know that someone out there was willing to buy subprime mortgage-backed securities without asking too many questions, they rushed to originate loans without checking the borrowers' creditworthiness, and credit quality deteriorated. But for a while, the problems were hidden by growing house prices and low defaults—easy credit masked the problems caused by easy credit—until house prices stopped rising and the flood of defaults burst forth."[2]

Who were these buyers? Table 1, reporting the number of NTMs outstanding on June 30, 2008, identified government agencies and private organizations required by the government to acquire, hold, or securitize NTMs as responsible for two-thirds of these mortgages, about 19 million. The table also identifies the private sector as the securitizer of the remaining third, about 7.8 million loans. In other words, if we are looking for the buyer of the NTMs that were being created by originators at the local level, the government's policies would seem to be the most likely culprit. The private sector certainly played a role, but it was a subordinate one. Moreover, what the private sector did was respond to demand—that's what the private sector does—but the government's role involved deliberate policy, an entirely different matter. Of its own volition, it created a demand that would not otherwise have been there.

The deterioration in mortgage standards did *not* occur—contrary to the Commission majority's apparent view—because banks and other originators suddenly started to make deficient loans; nor was it because of insufficient regulation at the originator level. The record shows unambiguously that government regulations made FHA, Fannie and Freddie, mortgage banks, and insured banks of all kinds into *competing* buyers. All of them needed NTMs in order to meet various government requirements. Fannie and Freddie were subject to increasingly stringent affordable housing requirements; FHA was tasked with insuring loans to low-income borrowers that would not be made unless insured; banks and S&Ls were required by CRA to show that they were also making loans to the same group of borrowers; mortgage bankers who signed up for the HUD Best Practices Initiative and the Clinton administration's National Homeownership Strategy were required to make the same kind of loans. Profit had nothing to do with the motivations of these firms; they were responding to government direction. Under these circumstances, it should be no surprise that underwriting standards declined as all of these organizations scrambled to acquire the same low-quality mortgages.

1. HUD's Central Role

In testimony before the House Financial Services Committee on April 14, 2010, Shaun Donovan, Secretary of Housing and Urban Development, said in reference to the GSEs: "Seeing their market share decline [between 2004 and 2006] as a result of [a] change of demand, the GSEs made the decision to widen their focus from safer prime loans and

---

2. Raghuram G. Rajan, *Fault Lines*, p. 44.

begin chasing the non-prime market, loosening long-standing underwriting and risk management standards along the way. This would be a fateful decision that not only proved disastrous for the companies themselves—but ultimately also for the American taxpayer."

Earlier, in its "Report to Congress on the Root Causes of the Foreclosure Crisis" in January 2010, HUD declared: "The serious financial troubles of the GSEs that led to their being placed into conservatorship by the Federal government provides strong testament to the fact that the GSEs were, indeed, overexposed to unduly risky mortgage investments. However, *the evidence suggests that the GSEs' decisions to purchase or guarantee non-prime loans was motivated much more by efforts to chase market share and profits than by the need to satisfy federal regulators.*"[3] [emphasis supplied]

Finger-pointing in Washington is endemic when problems occur, and agencies and individuals are constantly trying to find scapegoats for their own bad decisions, but HUD's effort to blame Fannie and Freddie for the decline in underwriting standards sets a new standard for running from responsibility. Contrast the 2010 statement quoted above with this statement by HUD in 2000, when it was significantly increasing Fannie and Freddie's affordable housing goals:

> Lower-income and minority families have made major gains in access to the mortgage market in the 1990s. A variety of reasons have accounted for these gains, including improved housing affordability, enhanced enforcement of the Community Reinvestment Act, *more flexible mortgage underwriting*, and stepped-up enforcement of the Fair Housing Act. *But most industry observers believe that one factor behind these gains has been the improved performance of Fannie Mae and Freddie Mac under HUD's affordable lending goals. HUD's recent increases in the goals for 2001–03 will encourage the GSEs to further step up their support for affordable lending.*[4] [emphasis supplied]

Or this statement in 2004, when HUD was again increasing the affordable housing goals for Fannie and Freddie:

> Millions of Americans with less than perfect credit or who cannot meet some of the tougher underwriting requirements of the prime market for reasons such as inadequate income documentation, limited downpayment or cash reserves, or the desire to take more cash out in a refinancing than conventional loans allow, rely on subprime lenders for access to mortgage financing. *If the GSEs reach deeper into the subprime market, more borrowers will benefit from the advantages that greater stability and standardization create.*[5] [emphasis supplied]

Or, finally, this statement in a 2005 report commissioned by HUD:

> More liberal mortgage financing has contributed to the increase in demand for housing. During the 1990s, lenders have been *encouraged by HUD and banking regulators*

---

3. Report to Congress on the Root Causes of the Foreclosure Crisis, January 2010, p. xii, http://www.huduser.org/portal/publications/hsgfin/foreclosure_09.html.

4. Issue Brief: HUD's Affordable Housing Goals for Fannie Mae and Freddie Mac, p. 5.

5. Final Rule, http://www.gpo.gov/fdsys/pkg/FR-2004-11-02/xml/FR-2004-11-02.xml.

to increase lending to low-income and minority households. The Community Reinvestment Act (CRA), Home Mortgage Disclosure Act (HMDA), government-sponsored enterprises (GSE) housing goals and fair lending laws have strongly encouraged mortgage brokers and lenders to market to low-income and minority borrowers. *Sometimes these borrowers are higher risk, with blemished credit histories and high debt or simply little savings for a downpayment. Lenders have responded with low downpayment loan products and automated underwriting, which has allowed them to more carefully determine the risk of the loan.*[6] [emphasis supplied]

Despite the recent effort by HUD to deny its own role in fostering the growth of sub-prime and other high-risk mortgage lending, there is strong—indeed irrefutable—evidence that, beginning in the early 1990s, HUD led an ultimately successful effort to lower underwriting standards in every area of the mortgage market where HUD had or could obtain influence. With support in congressional legislation, the policy was launched in the Clinton administration and extended almost to the end of the Bush administration. It involved FHA, which was under the direct control of HUD; Fannie Mae and Freddie Mac, which were subject to HUD's affordable housing regulations; and the mortgage banking industry, which—while not subject to HUD's legal jurisdiction—apparently agreed to pursue HUD's policies out of fear that they would be brought under the Community Reinvestment Act through legislation.[7] In addition, although not subject to HUD's jurisdiction, the new, tighter CRA regulations that became effective in 1995 led to a process in which community groups could obtain commitments for substantial amounts of CRA-qualifying mortgages and other loans to subprime borrowers when banks were applying for merger approvals.[8]

By 2004, HUD believed it had achieved the "revolution" it was looking for:

Over the past ten years, there has been a "revolution in affordable lending" that has extended homeownership opportunities to historically underserved households. Fannie Mae and Freddie Mac have been a substantial part of this "revolution in affordable lending." *During the mid-to-late 1990s, they added flexibility to their underwriting guidelines, introduced new low-downpayment products*, and worked to expand the use of automated underwriting in evaluating the creditworthiness of loan applicants. HMDA data suggest that the industry and GSE initiatives are increasing the flow of credit to underserved borrowers. *Between 1993 and 2003, conventional loans to low-income and minority families increased at much faster rates than loans to upper-income and nonminority families.*[9] [emphasis supplied]

---

6. HUD PDR, May 2005, HUD Contract C-OPC-21895, Task Order CHI-T0007, "Recent House Price Trends and Homeownership Affordability", p. 85.

7. Steve Cocheo, "Fair-Lending Pressure Builds," *ABA Banking Journal,* vol. 86, 1994, http://www.questia.com/googleScholar.qst?docId=5001707340.

8. See NCRC, *CRA Commitments*, 2007.

9. *Federal Register,* vol. 69, no. 211, November 2, 2004, Rules and Regulations, p. 63585, http://www.gpo.gov/fdsys/pkg/FR-2004-11-02/xml/FR-2004-11-02.xml.

This turned out to be an immense error of policy. By 2010, even the strongest supporters of affordable housing as enforced by HUD had recognized their error. In an interview on Larry Kudlow's CNBC television program in late August, Barney Frank—the chair of the House Financial Services Committee and previously the strongest congressional advocate for affordable housing—conceded that he had erred: "I hope by next year we'll have abolished Fannie and Freddie . . . it was a great mistake to push lower-income people into housing they couldn't afford and couldn't really handle once they had it." He then added, "I had been too sanguine about Fannie and Freddie."[10]

2. THE DECLINE OF MORTGAGE UNDERWRITING STANDARDS

Before the enactment of the GSE Act in 1992, and HUD's adoption of a policy thereafter to reduce underwriting standards, the GSEs followed conservative underwriting practices. For example, in a random review by Fannie Mae of 25,804 loans from October 1988 to January 1992, over 78 percent had LTV ratios of 80 percent or less, while only 5.75 percent had LTV ratios of 91 to 95 percent.[11] High-risk lending was confined primarily to FHA (which was controlled by HUD) and specialized subprime lenders who often sold the mortgages they originated to FHA. What caused these conservative standards to decline? The Commission majority, echoing Chairman Bernanke, seems to believe that the impetus was competition among the banks, irresponsibility among originators, and the desire for profit. The majority's report offers no other explanation.

However, there is no difficulty finding the source of the reductions in mortgage underwriting standards for Fannie and Freddie, or for the originators for whom they were the buyers. HUD made clear in numerous statements that its policy—in order to make credit available to low-income borrowers—was specifically *intended* to reduce underwriting standards. The GSE Act enabled HUD to put Fannie and Freddie into competition with FHA, and vice versa, creating what became a contest to lower mortgage standards. As the Fannie Mae Foundation noted in a 2000 report: "FHA loans constituted the largest share of Countrywide's [subprime lending] activity, until Fannie Mae and Freddie Mac began accepting loans with higher LTVs [loan-to-value ratios] and greater underwriting flexibilities."[12]

Under the GSE Act, the HUD Secretary was authorized to establish affordable housing goals for Fannie and Freddie. Congress required that these goals include a low- and

---

10. Larry Kudlow, "Barney Frank Comes Home to the Facts," GOPUSA, August 23, 2010, available at http://www.gopusa.com/commentary/2010/08/23/kudlow_barney_frank_comes_home_to_the_facts/ (accessed September 20, 2010).

11. Document in author's files.

12. Fannie Mae Foundation, "Making New Markets: Case Study of Countrywide Home Loans," 2000, http://content.knowledgeplex.org/kp2/programs/pdf/rep_newmortmkts_countrywide.pdf.

moderate-income goal and a special affordable goal (discussed below), both of which could be adjusted in the future. Among the factors the secretary was to consider in establishing the goals were national housing needs and "the ability of the enterprises [Fannie and Freddie] to lead the industry in making mortgage credit available for low-and moderate-income families." The act also established an interim affordable housing goal of 30 percent for the two-year period beginning January 1, 1993. Under this requirement, 30 percent of the GSEs' mortgage purchases had to be affordable housing loans, defined as loans to borrowers at or below the AMI.[13]

Further, the act established a "special affordable" goal to meet the "unaddressed needs of, and affordable to, low-income families in low-income areas and very low-income families." This category was defined as follows: "(i) 45 percent shall be mortgages of low-income families who live in census tracts in which the median income does not exceed 80 percent of the area median income; and (ii) 55 percent shall be mortgages of very low income families," which were later defined as 60 percent of AMI.[14] Although the GSE Act initially required that the GSEs spend on special affordable mortgages "not less than 1 percent of the dollar amount of the mortgage purchases by the [GSEs] for the previous year," HUD raised this requirement substantially in later years. Ultimately, it became the most difficult AH burden for Fannie and Freddie to meet.

Finally, the GSEs were directed to: "(A) assist primary lenders to make housing credit available in areas with low-income and minority families; and (B) assist insured depository institutions to meet their obligations under the Community Reinvestment Act of 1977."[15] There will be more on the CRA and its effect on the quality of mortgages later in this section.

Congress also made clear in the act that its intention was to call into question the high-quality underwriting guidelines of the time. It did so by directing Fannie and Freddie to "examine":

(1) The extent to which the underwriting guidelines prevent or inhibit the purchase or securitization of mortgages for houses in mixed-use, urban center, and predominantly minority neighborhoods and for housing for low- and moderate-income families;

(2) The standards employed by private mortgage insurers and the extent to which such standards inhibit the purchase and securitization by the enterprises of mortgages described in paragraph (1); and

(3) The implications of implementing underwriting standards that—
   (A) establish a downpayment requirement for mortgagors of 5 percent or less;
   (B) allow the use of cash on hand as a source of downpayments; and
   (C) approve borrowers who have a credit history of delinquencies if the borrower can demonstrate a satisfactory credit history for at least the 12-month period ending on the date of the application for the mortgage.[16]

---

13. GSE Act, Section 1332.
14. Id., Section 1333.
15. Id., Section 1335.
16. Id., Section 1354(a).

I could not find a record of reports by Fannie and Freddie required under this section of the act, but it would have been fairly clear to both companies, and to HUD, what Congress wanted in asking for these studies. Prevailing underwriting standards were inhibiting mortgage financing for low- and moderate-income families, and would have to be substantially relaxed in order to meet the goals of the act. Whatever the motivation, HUD set out to ensure that downpayment requirements were substantially reduced (eventually, they reached zero), and past credit history became a much less important issue when mortgages were made (permitting subprime mortgages to become far more common).

Until 1995, HUD enforced the temporary AH goals originally put in place by the GSE Act. With the exception of the special affordable requirements, which were small at this point, these goals were not burdensome. In the ordinary course of their business, the GSEs seem to have bought enough mortgages made to borrowers below the AMI to qualify for the 30 percent AH goal. In 1995, however, HUD raised the LMI goal to 40 percent, applicable to 1996, and to 42 percent for subsequent years. In terms of its effect on Fannie and Freddie, HUD's most important move at this time was to set a Special Affordable goal (low- and very-low-income borrowers) of 12 percent, which increased to 14 percent in 1997. Efforts to find loans to low- or very-low-income borrowers (80 percent and 60 percent of AMI, respectively) that did not involve high risks would prove difficult. As early as November 1995, even before the effect of these new and higher goals, Fannie's staff had already recognized that Fannie's Community Homebuyer Program (CHBP), which featured a 97 percent LTV ratio—i.e., 3 percent downpayment[17]—was showing significant rates of serious delinquency that exceeded Fannie's expected rates by 26 percent in origination year 1992, 93 percent in 1993, and 57 percent in 1994.[18]

In 1995, continuing its efforts to erode underwriting standards in order to increase homeownership, HUD issued a policy statement entitled "The National Homeownership Strategy: Partners in the American Dream." The Strategy was prepared by HUD, "under the direction of Secretary Henry G. Cisneros, in response to a request from President Clinton."[19] The first paragraph of chapter 1 stated: "The purpose of the National Homeownership Strategy is to achieve an all-time high level of homeownership in America within the next 6 years through an unprecedented collaboration of public and private housing industry organizations."

The Strategy paper then noted that "industry representatives agreed to the formation of working groups to help develop the National Homeownership Strategy" and made clear that one of its purposes was to increase homeownership by reducing downpayments: "*Lending institutions, secondary market investors, mortgage insurers, and other members of the partnership should work collaboratively to reduce homebuyer downpayment requirements.* Mortgage financing with high loan-to-value ratios should generally be associated with enhanced homebuyer counseling and, where available, supplemental sources of downpayment

---

17. Fannie Mae, "Opening Doors with Fannie Mae's Community Lending Products," 1995, p.3.

18. Fannie Mae, Memo from Credit Policy Staff to Credit Policy Committee, "CHBP Performance," November 14, 1995, p. 1.

19. HUD, "The National Homeownership Strategy: Partners in the American Dream," available at http://web.archive.org/web/20010106203500/www.huduser.org/publications/affhsg/homeown/chap1.html.

assistance."[20] According to a HUD summary, the purpose of the Strategy was to make financing "more available, affordable, and flexible."[21] [emphasis supplied] It continued:

The inability (either real or perceived) of many younger families to qualify for a mortgage is widely recognized as a very serious barrier to homeownership. The National Homeownership Strategy commits both government and the mortgage industry to a number of initiatives designed to:

Cut transaction costs through streamlined regulations and technological and procedural efficiencies.

Reduce downpayment requirements and interest costs by making terms more flexible, providing subsidies to low- and moderate-income families, and creating incentives to save for homeownership.

Increase the availability of alternative financing products in housing markets throughout the country.[22] [emphasis supplied]

Reductions in downpayments, the area on which HUD particularly concentrated in pursuing its AH goals and the National Homeownership Strategy, are especially important in weakening underwriting standards. Table 4, below, based on a large sample of loans from the 1990s, shows the risk relationships between downpayments and mortgage risks. It is particularly instructive to note that when low downpayments (i.e., high LTVs) are combined with low FICO scores (subprime loans), the expected delinquencies and defaults are multiplied several fold. For example, when a loan with a FICO score below 620 is combined with a downpayment of 5 percent, the risk of default is 4.2 times greater than it would be if the downpayment were 25 percent.

Despite these obvious dangers, HUD saw the erosion of downpayment requirements imposed by the private sector as one of the keys to the success of its strategy to increase home ownership through the "partnership" it had established with the mortgage financing community: "The amount of borrower equity is an important factor in assessing mortgage loan quality. *However, many low-income families do not have access to sufficient funds for a downpayment. While members of the partnership have already made significant strides in reducing this barrier to home purchase, more must be done.* In 1989 only 7 percent of home mortgages were made with less than 10 percent downpayment. By August 1994, low downpayment mortgage loans had increased to 29 percent."[23] [emphasis supplied]

HUD's policy was highly successful in achieving the goals it sought. In 1989, only 1 in 230 homebuyers bought a home with a downpayment of 3 percent or less, but by 2003, 1 in 7 buyers was providing a downpayment at that level, and by 2007, the number was less

20. Id., Chapter 4, Action 35.

21. The term "flexible" has a special meaning when HUD uses it. See note 5, part I.

22. HUD, Urban Policy Brief No.2, August 1995, available at http://www.huduser.org/publications/txt/hdbrf2.txt.

23. HUD's "National Homeownership Strategy–Partners in the American Dream," http://web.archive.org/web/20010106203500/www.huduser.org/publications/affhsg/homeown/chap1.html.

TABLE 4
HIGH LTVs ENHANCE THE RISK OF LOW FICO SCORES

	Column 1	Column 2	Column 3	Column 4	Column 5	Column 6
Row 1	FICO Score	≤ 70% LTV	71–80% LTV	81–90% LTV	91–95% LTV	Relation of Column 5 to Column 3
Row 2	< 620	1.0	4.8	11	20	4.2 times
Row 3	620–679	0.5	2.3	5.3	9.4	4.1 times
Row 4	680–720	0.2	1.0	2.3	4.1	4.1 times
Row 5	> 720	0.1	0.4	0.9	1.6	4 times

SOURCE: "Deconstructing the Subprime Debacle Using New Indices of Underwriting Quality and Economic Conditions: A First Look," by Anderson, Capozza, and Van Order, found at http://www.ufanet.com/DeconstructingSubprimeJuly2008.pdf.

than 1 in 3. The gradual increase in LTVs and CLTVs (first and second loans combined to produce a lower downpayment) under HUD's policies is shown in figure 4. Note the date (1992) when HUD began to have some influence over the downpayments that the GSEs would accept.

That HUD's AH goals were the reason Fannie increased its high-LTV (low downpayment) lending is clearly described in a Fannie presentation to HUD assistant secretary Albert Trevino on January 10, 2003: "Analyses of the market demonstrate the greatest barrier to home ownership for most renters are related to wealth—the lack of money for a downpayment . . . our low-downpayment lending—negligible until 1994—has grown considerably. It is a key part of our strategy to serve low-income and minority borrowers." The chart that accompanied that statement showed that Fannie's home purchase loans over 95 percent LTV had increased from one percent in 1994 to 7.9 percent in 2001.[24]

The close relationship between low downpayments and delinquencies and defaults on mortgages is shown in figure 5, which compares the increase in FHA 97 percent (or greater) CLTV or LTV mortgages to the increase in the foreclosure start rate on all loans published by the Mortgage Bankers Association.

In 1995, HUD also ruled that Fannie and Freddie could get AH credit for buying PMBS that were backed by loans to low-income borrowers.[25] This provided an opportunity for subprime lenders to create pools of subprime mortgages that were likely to be AH goals-rich. These were then sold through Wall Street underwriters to Fannie and Freddie, which became the largest buyers of these high-risk PMBS between 2002 and 2005.[26] These PMBS pools were not bought for profit. As Adolfo Marzol, Fannie's Chief Credit Officer, noted to Fannie CEO Dan Mudd in a 2005 memorandum: "Large 2004 private label [PMBS] volumes were necessary to achieve challenging minority lending goals and housing goals."[27] There

24. "Fannie Mae's Role in Affordable Housing Finance: Connecting World Capital Markets and America's Homebuyers," Presentation to HUD Assistant Secretary Albert Trevino, January 10, 2003.

25. http://www.washingtonpost.com/wp-dyn/content/article/2008/06/09/AR2008060902626.html.

26. See note 26, part I.

27. Fannie Mae internal memo, Adolfo Marzol to Dan Mudd, "RE: Private Label Securities," March 2, 2005.

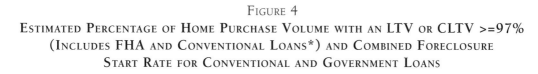

FIGURE 4

ESTIMATED PERCENTAGE OF HOME PURCHASE VOLUME WITH AN **LTV** OR **CLTV** >=97%
(INCLUDES **FHA** AND CONVENTIONAL LOANS*) AND COMBINED FORECLOSURE
START RATE FOR CONVENTIONAL AND GOVERNMENT LOANS

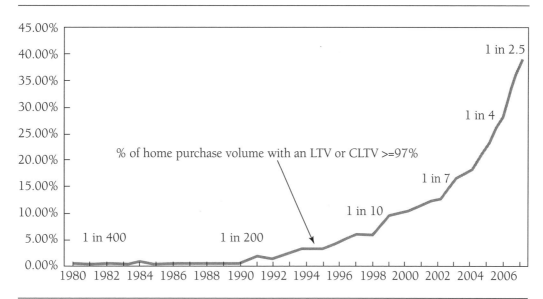

SOURCES: FHA 2009 Actuarial Study, and HUD"s Office of Policy Development and Research—Profiles of GSE Mortgage Purchases in 1999 and 2000, in 2001–2004, and in 2005–2007, and Fannie's 2007 10-K. Compiled by Edward Pinto. NOTE: * = Fannie's percentage of home purchase loans with an LTV or CLTV >–97% used as the proxy for conventional loans.

is a strong possibility that by creating a market for PMBS backed by NTMs, Fannie and Freddie enabled Wall Street—which had previously focused on securitizing prime jumbo loans—to get its start in developing an underwriting business in PMBS based on NTMs.

HUD pursued these policies throughout the balance of the Clinton administration and into the administration of George W. Bush. Ultimately, they would lead to the mortgage meltdown in 2007, as vast numbers of mortgages with low or no downpayments and other nontraditional features suffused the financial system. But in June 1995, the dangers in HUD's policies were not recognized. As President Clinton said in a 1995 speech: "Our homeownership strategy will not cost the taxpayers one extra red cent. It will not require legislation. It will not add more federal programs or grow the Federal bureaucracy."[28] The lesson here is that the government can accomplish a lot of its goals without growing, as long as it has the power to enlist the private sector. That does not mean, however, as we have all now learned, that the taxpayers will not ultimately be faced with the costs.

The next significant move in the AH goals was made under HUD Secretary Andrew Cuomo, and it was a major step. On July 29, 1999, HUD issued a press release with the heading "Cuomo Announces Action to Provide $2.4 trillion in Mortgages for Affordable Housing for 28.1 Million Families."[29] The release began: "Housing and Urban Development

---

28. William J. Clinton, Remarks on the National Homeownership Strategy, June 5, 1995.
29. HUD Press Release, HUD No. 99-131, July 29, 1999.

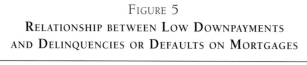

FIGURE 5
RELATIONSHIP BETWEEN LOW DOWNPAYMENTS
AND DELINQUENCIES OR DEFAULTS ON MORTGAGES

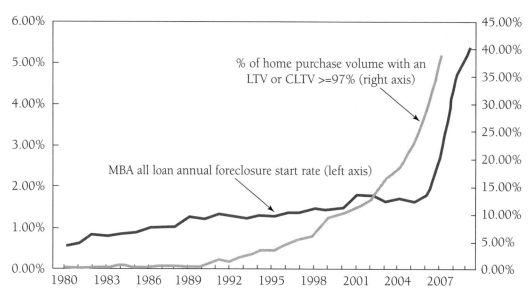

SOURCES: MBA National Delinquency Survey, FHA 2009 Actuarial Study, and HUD"s Office of Policy Development and Research—Profiles of GSE Mortgage Purchases in 1999 and 2000, in 2001–2004, and in 2005–2007, SMR's "Piggyback Mortgage Lending," and Fannie's 2007 10-K. Fannie is used as the proxy on the conventional market. Compiled by Edward Pinto.

Secretary Andrew Cuomo today announced a policy to require the nation's two largest housing finance companies to buy $2.4 trillion in mortgages over the next 10 years to provide affordable housing for about 28.1 million low- and moderate-income families." This was followed by a quote from President Clinton to emphasize the importance of the initiative: "During the last six and a half years, my Administration has put tremendous emphasis on promoting homeownership and making housing more affordable for all Americans. . . . Today, the homeownership rate is at an all-time high, with more than 66 percent of all American families owning their homes. Today, we take another significant step."

The release then pointed out that the AH goals would be substantially raised and that "[u]nder the higher goals, Fannie Mae and Freddie Mac will buy an additional $488.3 billion in mortgages that will be used to provide affordable housing for 7 million more low- and moderate-income families over the next 10 years. Those new mortgages and families are over and above the $1.9 trillion in mortgages for 21.1 million families that would have been generated if the current goals had been retained." The release also noted that "Fannie Mae Chairman Franklin D. Raines joined Cuomo at the news conference in which Cuomo announced the HUD action. Raines committed Fannie Mae to reaching HUD's increased Affordable Housing goals."

The policy behind this substantial increase in the AH goals was expressed in HUD's discussion of the rule-making: "To fulfill the intent of [the GSE Act], the GSEs should lead the industry in ensuring that access to mortgage credit is made available for very low-, low- and moderate-income families and residents of underserved areas. HUD recognizes that, to lead the mortgage industry over time, *the GSEs will have to stretch to reach certain goals and close the gap between the secondary mortgage market and the primary mortgage market. This approach is consistent with Congress' recognition that 'the enterprises will need to stretch their efforts to achieve' the goals.*"[30] [emphasis supplied]

The new AH goals announced in 1999 were not finally issued until October 2000. Their specifics were stunning and drove Fannie and Freddie into a new and far more challenging era. The basic goal, an LMI requirement of 42 percent, was raised to 50 percent, and the special affordable goal was raised from 14 percent to 20 percent. As a result, 75 percent of the increase in goals was concentrated in the low- and very-low-income category—where the risks were the greatest. A HUD memo summarized the new rules:[31]

For each year from 2001 through 2003, the goals are:

- *Low- and moderate-income goal.* At least 50 percent of the dwelling units financed by each GSE's mortgage purchases should be for families with incomes no greater than area median income (AMI), defined as median income for the metropolitan area or nonmetropolitan county. The corresponding goal was 42 percent for 1997–2000.
- *Special affordable goal.* At least 20 percent of the dwelling units financed by each GSE's mortgage purchases should be for very low-income families (those with incomes no greater than 60 percent of AMI) or for low-income families (those with incomes no greater than 80 percent of LMI) in low-income areas. The corresponding goal was 14 percent for 1997–2000.
- *Underserved areas goal.* At least 31 percent of the dwelling units financed by each GSE's mortgage purchases should be for units located in underserved areas. Research by HUD and others has demonstrated that low-income and high-minority census tracts have high mortgage denial rates and low mortgage origination rates, and this forms the basis for HUD's definition of underserved areas. The corresponding goal was 24 percent for 1997–2000.

HUD's new and more stringent AH goal requirements immediately stimulated strong interest at the GSEs for CRA loans, substantial portions of which were likely to be goals-qualifying. This is evident in a speech by Fannie's Vice Chair, Jamie Gorelick, to an American Bankers Association conference on October 30, 2000, just after HUD announced the latest increase in the AH goals for the GSEs:

Your CRA business is very important to us. Since 1997, we have done nearly $7 billion in specially targeted CRA business—all with depositories like yours. But that is just the beginning. Before the decade is over, Fannie Mae is committed to finance

30. http://frwebgate.access.gpo.gov/cgi-bin/getdoc.cgi?dbname=2000_register&docid=page+65043-65092.
31. HUD, Office of Policy Development and Research, Issue Brief No. 5, January 2001, p. 3.

over $20 billion in specially targeted CRA business and over $500 billion in CRA business altogether. . . .

We want your CRA loans because they help us meet our housing goals...we will buy them from your portfolios, or package them into securities . . . We will also purchase CRA mortgages you make right at the point of origination. . . . You can originate CRA loans for our purchase with one of our CRA-friendly products, like our 3 percent down Fannie 97. Or we have special community lending products with flexible underwriting and special financing. . . . Our approach is "CRA your way."[32]

The 50 percent level in the new HUD regulations was a turning point. Fannie and Freddie had to stretch a bit to reach the previous goal of 42 percent, but 50 percent was a significant challenge. As Dan Mudd told the Commission,

Fannie Mae's mission regulator, HUD, imposed ever-higher housing goals that were very difficult to meet during my tenure as CEO [2005–2008]. The HUD goals greatly impacted Fannie Mae's business, as a great deal of time, resources, energy, and personnel were dedicated to finding ways to meet these goals. HUD increased the goals aggressively over time to the point where they exceeded the 50% mark, requiring Fannie Mae to place greater emphasis on purchasing loans to underserved areas. Fannie Mae had to devote a great deal of resources to running its business to satisfy HUD's goals and subgoals.[33]

Mudd's point can be illustrated with simple arithmetic. At the 50 percent level, for every mortgage acquired that was not goal-qualifying, Fannie and Freddie had to acquire a goal-qualifying loan. Although about 30 percent of prime loans were likely to be goal-qualifying in any event (because they were made to borrowers at or below the applicable AMI), most prime loans were not. Subprime and other NTM loans were goals-rich, but not every such loan was goal-qualifying. Accordingly, in order to meet a 50 percent goal, the GSEs had to purchase ever-larger amounts of goals-rich NTMs in order to acquire sufficient quantities of goals-qualifying loans.

Thus, in a presentation to HUD in 2004, Fannie argued that to meet a 57 percent LMI goal (which was under consideration by HUD at the time) it would have to acquire 151.5 percent more subprime loans than the goal in order to capture enough goal-qualifying loans.[34] Moreover, with the special affordable category at 20 percent in 2004, the GSEs had to acquire large numbers of NTM loans from borrowers who were at or below 60 percent of the AMI. This requirement drove Fannie and Freddie even further into risk territory in search of loans that would meet this subgoal.

32. Jamie S. Gorelick, Remarks at American Bankers Association conference, October 30, 2000, http://web.archive.org/web/20011120061407/www.fanniemae.com/news/speeches/speech_152.html.

33. Daniel H. Mudd's Responses to the Questions Presented in the FCIC's June 3, 2010, Letter, Answer to Question 6: How influential were HUD's affordable housing guidelines in Fannie Mae's purchase of subprime and Alt-A loans? Were Alt-A loans "goals-rich"? Were Alt-A loans net positive for housing goals?

34. Fannie Mae, "Discussion of HUD's Proposed Housing Goals," Presentation to the Department of Housing and Urban Development, June 9, 2004.

Most of what was going on here was under the radar, even for specialists in the housing finance field, but not everyone missed it. In a paper published in 2001,[35] financial analyst Josh Rosner recognized the deterioration in mortgage standards, although he did not recognize how many loans were subject to this problem:

> Over the past decade Fannie Mae and Freddie Mac have reduced required down payments on loans that they purchase in the secondary market. Those requirements have declined from 10% to 5% to 3% and in the past few months Fannie Mae announced that it would follow Freddie Mac's recent move into the 0% down payment mortgage market. Although they are buying low down payment loans, those loans must be insured with "private mortgage insurance" (PMI). On homes with PMI, even the closing costs can now be borrowed through unsecured loans, gifts or subsidies. This means that not only can the buyer put zero dollars down to purchase a new house but also that the mortgage can finance the closing costs. . . .
>
> *[I]t appears a large portion of the housing sector's growth in the 1990's came from the easing of the credit underwriting process.* . . . The virtuous cycle of increasing homeownership due to greater leverage has the potential to become a vicious cycle of lower home prices due to an accelerating rate of foreclosures.[36] [emphasis supplied]

The last increase in the AH goals occurred in 2004, when HUD raised the LMI goal to 52 percent for 2005, 53 percent for 2006, 55 percent for 2007, and 56 percent for 2008. Again, the percentage increases in the special affordable category outstripped the general LMI goal, putting added pressure on Fannie and Freddie to acquire additional risky NTMs. This category increased from 20 percent to 27 percent over that period. In the release that accompanied the increases, HUD declared:

> Millions of Americans with less than perfect credit or who cannot meet some of the tougher underwriting requirements of the prime market for reasons such as inadequate income documentation, limited downpayment or cash reserves, or the desire to take more cash out in a refinancing than conventional loans allow, rely on subprime lenders for access to mortgage financing. *If the GSEs reach deeper into the subprime market,* more borrowers will benefit from the advantages that greater stability and standardization create.[37] [emphasis supplied]

Fannie did indeed reach deeper into the subprime market, confirming in a March 2003 presentation to HUD: "Higher goals force us deeper into FHA and subprime."[38] According to HUD data, as a result of the AH goals, Fannie Mae's acquisitions of goal-qualifying loans (which were primarily subprime and Alt-A) increased (i) for very-low-income borrowers from 5.2 percent of their acquisitions in 1993 to 12.2 percent in 2007; (ii) for

35. Josh Rosner, "Housing in the New Millennium: A Home Without Equity Is Just a Rental With Debt," June, 2001, p. 7, available at http://papers.ssrn.com/sol3/papers.cfm?abstract_id=1162456.

36. Id., p. 29.

37. http://www.gpo.gov/fdsys/pkg/FR-2004-11-02/xml/FR-2004-11-02.xml, p. 63601.

38. Fannie Mae, "The HUD Housing Goals", March 2003.

special affordable borrowers from 6.4 percent in 1993 to 15.2 percent in 2007; and (iii) for less-than-median-income borrowers (which includes the other two categories) from 29.2 percent in 1993 to 41.5 percent in 2007.[39]

By 2004, Fannie and Freddie were sufficiently in need of subprime loans to meet the AH goals that their CEOs, as the following account shows, went to a meeting of mortgage bankers to ask for more subprime loan production:

> The top executives of Freddie Mac and Fannie Mae [Richard Syron and Franklin Raines] made no bones about their interest in buying loans made to borrowers formerly considered the province of nonprime and other niche lenders. . . . Fannie Mae Chairman and [CEO] Franklin Raines told mortgage bankers in San Francisco that his company's lender-customers "need to learn the best from the subprime market and bring the best from the prime market into [the subprime market]." He offered praise for nonprime lenders that, he said, "are some of the best marketers in financial services." . . . *"We have to push products and opportunities to people who have lesser credit quality,"* he said.[40] [emphasis supplied]

Accordingly, by 2004, when HUD put new and tougher AH goals into effect, Fannie and Freddie were using every available resource to meet the goals, including subprime loans, Alt-A loans, and the purchase of PMBS. Some observers, including the Commission's majority, have claimed that the GSEs bought NTM loans and PMBS for profit—that these instruments did not assist Fannie and Freddie in meeting the AH goals and therefore must have been acquired because they were profitable. However, the statement by Adolfo Marzol reported above, and the data in table 5, furnished to the Commission by Fannie Mae, show that all three categories of NTMs—subprime loans (i.e., loans to borrowers with FICO scores less than 660), Alt-A loans, and PMBS (called PLS for "Private Label Securities" in the table)—fulfilled the AH goals or subgoals for the years and in the percentages shown below. (Bolded numbers exceeded the applicable goal.) Table 5 also shows, significantly, that the gradual increase in Fannie's purchases of these NTMs closely followed the gradual increase in the goals between 1996 and 2008.

Table 5 also shows that ordinary subprime loans, Alt-A loans, and PMBS backed by subprime loans were not always sufficient to meet the AH goals. For this reason, Fannie

---

39. HUD, Office of Policy Development and Research, Profiles of GSE Mortgage Purchases, 1992–2000, 2001–2004, and 2005–2007.

40. Neil Morse, "Looking for New Customers," *Mortgage Banking*, December 1, 2004. It may be significant that the chairman of Freddie Mac at the time, Leland Brendsel, did not attend the press conference or pledge support for HUD's new goals. Raines must have forgotten his 1999 pledge to Secretary Cuomo and his speech to the mortgage bankers when he wrote in a letter to the *Wall Street Journal* on August 3, 2010: "The facts about the financial collapse of Fannie and Freddie are pretty clear and a matter of public record. The company managers, their regulator and the Treasury have all said that the losses which crippled the companies were caused by the purchase of loans with lower credit standards between 2005 and 2007. The companies explicitly changed their credit standards in order to regain market share after Wall Street began to define market credit standards in 2004."

TABLE 5
NONTRADITIONAL MORTGAGES AND THE AFFORDABLE HOUSING GOALS

	Low- & Moderate-Income Base Goal		Special Affordable Base Goal		Underserved Base Goal	
Year	Actual*	Goal	Actual*	Goal	Actual*	Goal
Credit Score <660 Originations						
1996	38.08%	40 %	**12.31%**	12%	**32.10%**	21%
1997	38.04%	42%	12.35%	14%	**33.03%**	24%
1998	37.72%	42%	11.76%	14%	**29.37%**	24%
1999	40.36%	42%	**14.04%**	14%	**30.87%**	24%
2000	**43.69%**	42%	**17.83%**	14%	**35.79%**	24%
2001	45.98%	50%	17.90%	20%	**34.91%**	31%
2002	49.66%	50%	**20.09%**	20%	**37.29%**	31%
2003	49.18%	50%	19.38%	20%	**34.12%**	31%
2004	**52.71%**	50%	**22.14%**	20%	**37.54%**	31%
2005	**54.39%**	52%	**24.21%**	22%	**44.38%**	37%
2006	**56.34%**	53%	**25.85%**	23%	**46.34%**	38%
2007	**55.47%**	55%	24.76%	25%	**46.45%**	38%
2008	55.24%	56%	25.50%	27%	**45.39%**	39%
Alt-A Originations						
1999	**48.83%**	42%	**24.17%**	14%	**37.41%**	24%
2000	40.61%	42%	**18.74%**	14%	**41.03%**	24%
2001	39.05%	50%	16.41%	20%	**40.66%**	31%
2002	42.77%	50%	18.13%	20%	**40.08%**	31%
2003	42.42%	50%	16.81%	20%	**37.34%**	31%
2004	44.13%	50%	18.56%	20%	**40.08%**	31%
2005	43.12%	52%	18.57%	22%	**45.36%**	37%
2006	40.43%	53%	18.09%	23%	**46.40%**	38%
2007	39.02%	55%	17.29%	25%	**50.29%**	38%
2008	42.37%	56%	18.52%	27%	**42.10%**	39%
PLS Backed by Subprime						
2003	**51.43%**	50%	19.57%	20%	**47.09%**	31%
2004^						
2005	50.95%	52%	19.86%	22%	**61.13%**	37%
2006	**60.63%**	53%	**23.51%**	23%	**60.12%**	38%
2007	52.96%	55%	19.21%	25%	**54.55%**	38%
2008	51.42%	56%	17.68%	27%	**64.45%**	39%

SOURCE: Fannie Mae, disk produced for FCIC, April 7, 2000.
NOTES: Throughout this analysis, I have not discussed the GSEs' compliance with the "Underserved Base Goal," which is included in this table. The Underserved Base Goal applied mostly to minorities and involved a different set of lending decisions than the LMI goal and the Special Affordable Goal. * = % of unit financed that qualified for base goals. ^ = Not included in housing goals scoring in 2004.

TABLE 6
HIGHER-RISK LOANS PRODUCED HIGHER DELINQUENCY RATES AT FANNIE MAE

	Goals by Vintage	Loan Count	Serious Delinquency Rate
2004 & Prior	EA/MCM & Housing Goals	115,686	17.59%
2005	EA/MCM & Housing Goals	56,822	22.35%
2006	EA/MCM & Housing Goals	110,539	25.19%
2007	EA/MCM & Housing Goals	224,513	29.70%

SOURCE: Fannie Mae, "GSE Credit Losses," presentation to House Financial Services Committee, April 16, 2010.

developed special categories of loans in which the firm waived some of its regular underwriting requirements in order to supplement what they were getting from higher quality NTMs. The two principal categories were My Community Mortgage (MCM) and Expanded Approval (EA). In many cases, these two categories enabled Fannie to meet the AH goals, but at the cost of much higher delinquency rates than occurred among higher-quality NTMs they acquired. As the years progressed and the AH goals increased, Fannie had to acquire increasing numbers of loans in these categories, and as shown in table 6, these increasing numbers also exhibited increasing delinquency rates:

Just how desperate Fannie and Freddie were to meet their AH goals is revealed by Fannie's behavior in 2004. As reported in the *American Banker* on May 13, 2005: "A House Financial Services Committee report shared with lawmakers Thursday accused Fannie Mae and Freddie Mac of engaging over several years in a series of dubious transactions to meet their affordable-housing goals. . . . The report cited several large transactions entered into by Fannie under which sellers were allowed to repurchase loans without recourse. For example, it said that in September 2003, Fannie bought the option to buy up to $12 billion of multifamily mortgage loans from Washington Mutual, Inc., for a fee of $2 million, the report said. Under the agreement, the GSE permitted WaMu to repurchase the loans. . . This was the largest multifamily transaction ever undertaken by Fannie Mae and was critical for Fannie Mae to reach the affordable-housing goals, the report said."[41]

A clearer statement of what happened here is contained in WaMu's 10-K for 2003. Freddie had engaged in a similar, but larger, transaction with WaMu in 2003, reported as follows in WaMu's 10-K dated December 31, 2003:

> Other noninterest income increased in 2003 compared with 2002 partially due to fees paid to the Company [WaMu] by the Federal Home Loan Mortgage Corporation ("FHLMC" or "Freddie Mac"). The Company received $100 million in nonrefundable fees to induce the Company to swap approximately $6 billion of multi-family loans for 100% of the beneficial interest in those loans in the form of mortgage-backed securities issued by Freddie Mac. Since the Company has the unilateral right to collapse the securities after one year, the Company has effectively retained control over the loans. Accordingly, the assets continue to be accounted

---

41. Rob Blackwell, "Two GSEs Cut Corners to Hit Goals, Report Says," *American Banker*, May 13, 2005, p. 1.

for and reported as loans. This transaction was undertaken by Freddie Mac in order to facilitate fulfilling its 2003 affordable housing goals as set by the Department of Housing and Urban Development.

Fannie and Freddie were both paying holders of mortgages to temporarily transfer to them possession of goal-qualifying loans that the GSEs could use to satisfy the AH goals for the year 2003. After the end of the year, the seller had an absolute right to reacquire these loans. There can be little doubt, then, that as early as 2003, Fannie and Freddie were under so much pressure to find the subprime or other loans that they needed to meet their affordable housing obligations that they were willing to pay substantial sums to window-dress their reports to HUD.

3. THE AFFORDABLE HOUSING GOALS WERE THE SOLE REASON THAT THE GSEs ACQUIRED SO MANY NTMs

Up to this point, we have seen that HUD's policy was to reduce underwriting standards in order to make mortgage credit more readily available to low-income borrowers, and that Fannie and Freddie not only took the AH goals seriously but were willing to go to extraordinary lengths to make sure that they met them. Nevertheless, it seems to have become an accepted idea in some quarters—including in the Commission majority's report—that Fannie and Freddie bought large numbers of subprime and Alt-A loans between 2004 and 2007 in order to recover the market share they had lost to subprime lenders such as Countrywide or Wall Street, or in order to make profits. Although there is no evidence whatever for this belief—and a great deal of evidence to the contrary—it has become another urban myth, repeated so often in books, blogs, and other media that it has attained a kind of reality.[42]

The formulations of the idea vary a bit. As noted earlier, HUD has claimed—absurdly, in light of its earlier efforts to reduce mortgage underwriting standards—that the GSEs were "chasing the nonprime market" or "chasing market share and profits," principally between 2004 and 2007. The inference, all too easily accepted, is that this is another example of private greed doing harm, but it is clear that HUD was simply trying to evade its own culpability for using the AH goals to degrade the GSEs' mortgage underwriting standards over the fifteen-year period between 1992 and 2007. The Commission majority also adopted a

---

42. See, e.g., Barry Ritholtz, "Get Me ReWrite!" in *Bailout Nation, Bailouts, Credit, Real Estate, Really, Really Bad Calls,* May 13, 2010, http://www.ritholtz.com/blog/2010/05/rewriting-the-causes-of-the-credit-crisis/print/; Dean Baker, "NPR Tells Us that Republicans Believe that Fannie and Freddie Caused the Crash" *Beat the Press Blog,* Center for Economic and Policy Research, http://www.cepr.net/index.php/blogs/beat-the-press/npr-tells-us-that-republicans-believe-that-fannie-and-freddie-caused-the-crash; Charles Duhigg, "Roots of the Crisis," *Frontline,* Feb 17, 2009, http://www.pbs.org/wgbh/pages/frontline/meltdown/themes/howwegothere.html.

version of this idea in its report, blaming the GSEs' loosening of their underwriting standards on a desire to please stock market analysts and investors, as well as to increase management compensation. None of HUD's statements about its efforts to reduce underwriting standards managed to make it into the Commission majority's report, which relied entirely on the idea that the GSEs' underwriting standards were reduced by their desire to "follow Wall Street and other lenders in [the] rush for fool's gold."

These claims place the blame for Fannie and Freddie's insolvency—and the huge number of low-quality mortgages in the U.S. financial system immediately prior to the financial crisis—on the firms' managements. They absolve the government, particularly HUD, from responsibility. The GSEs' managements made plenty of mistakes—and won't be defended here—but taking risks to compete for market share was not something they actually did. Because of the AH goals, Fannie and Freddie were major buyers of NTMs well before Wall Street firms and the subprime lenders who came to dominate the business entered the subprime PMBS market in any significant way. Moreover, the GSEs did not (indeed, could not) appreciably increase their purchases of NTMs during the years 2005 and 2006, when they had lost market share to the real PMBS issuers, Countrywide, and other subprime lenders.

The following discussion addresses each of the claims about the GSEs' motives in turn, and in the end will show that the only plausible motive for their actions was their effort to comply with HUD's AH goals.

Did the GSEs Acquire NTMs to "Compete for Market Share" with Wall Street or Others?

The idea that Fannie and Freddie were newcomers to the purchase of NTMs between 2004 and 2007—and reduced their underwriting standards so they could compete for market share with Wall Street or others—is wrong. As shown in table 7, the GSEs' acquisition of subprime loans and other NTMs began in the 1990s, when they first became subject to the AH goals. Research shows that, in contravention of their earlier standards, the GSEs began to acquire high-LTV mortgages in 1994, shortly after the enactment of the GSE Act and the imposition of the AH goals, and by 2001—before the PMBS market reached $100 billion in annual issuances—the GSEs had already acquired at least $700 billion in NTMs, including over $400 billion in subprime loans.[43] Far from following Wall Street or anyone else into subprime loans between 2004 and 2007, the GSEs had become the largest buyers of subprime and other NTMs many years before the PMBS market began to develop. Given these facts, it would be more accurate to say that Wall Street and the subprime lenders who later came to dominate the PMBS market followed the GSEs into subprime lending. Table 7 does not show any significant increase in the GSEs' acquisition of NTMs from 2004 to 2007, and the amount of subprime PMBS they acquired during this period actually decreased. This is consistent with the fact—outlined below—that the GSEs did not make any special effort to compete for market share during these years.

---

43. Pinto, "Government Housing Policies in the Lead-Up to the Financial Crisis: A Forensic Study," Chart 52, p. 148, http://www.aei.org/docLib/Government-Housing-Policies-Financial-Crisis-Pinto-102110.pdf.

TABLE 7
GSE PURCHASES OF SUBPRIME AND ALT-A LOANS

$ in billions	1997	1998	1999	2000	2001	2002	2003	2004	2005	2006	2007	1997–2007
Subprime PMBS	$3*	$18*	$18*	$11*	$16*	$38	$82	$180	$169	$110	$62	$707
Subprime loans**	$37	$83	$74	$65	$159	$206	$262	$144	$139	$138	$195	$1,502
Alt-A PMBS	Unk.	Unk.	Unk.	Unk.	Unk.	$18	$12	$30	$36	$43	$15	$154
Alt-A loans***	Unk.	Unk.	Unk.	Unk.	Unk.	$66	$77	$64	$77	$157	$178	$619
High-LTV loans****	$32	$44	$62	$61	$84	$87	$159	$123	$126	$120	$226	$1,124
Total*****	$72	$145	$154	$137	$259	$415	$592	$541	$547	$568	$676	$4,106

SOURCE: Pinto, "Government Housing Policies in the Lead-up to the Financial Crisis: A Forensic Study," Chart 52, p. 148, http://www.aei.org/docLib/Government-Housing-Policies-Financial-Crisis-Pinto-102110.pdf.
NOTES:
* = Total purchases of PMBS for 1997–2001 are known. Subprime purchases for these years were estimated based upon the percentage that subprime PMBS constituted of total PMBS purchases in 2002 (57%).
** = Loans where borrower's FICO <660.
*** = Fannie and Freddie used their various affordable housing programs and individual lender variance programs (many times in conjunction with their automated underwriting systems once these came into general use in the late-1990s) to approve loans with Alt-A characteristics. However, they generally did not classify these loans as Alt-A. Classification as Alt-A started in the early 1990s. There is an unknown number of additional loans that had higher debt ratios, reduced reserves, loosened credit requirements, expanded seller contributions, etc. The volume of these loans is not included.
**** = Loans with an original LTV or original combined LTV >90% (given industry practices, this effectively means >=95%). Data to estimate loans with CLTV >90% are unavailable prior to 2003. Amounts for 2003–2007 are grossed up by 60% to account for the impact of loans with a CLTV >90%. These estimates are based on disclosures by Fannie and Freddie that at the end of 2007 their total exposures to loans with an LTV or CLTV >90% was 50% and 75% percent, respectively, higher than their exposure to loans with an LTV >90%. Fannie reports on p. 128 of its 2007 10-K that 15% of its entire book had an original combined LTV >90%. Its Original LTV percentage >90% (without counting the impact of any 2nd mortgage simultaneously negotiated) is 9.9%. Freddie reports on p. 60 of its Q2:2008 10-Q that 14% of its portfolio had an original combined LTV >90%. Its OLTV percentage >90% (without counting any simultaneous 2nd) is 8%. While Fannie and Freddie purchased only the first mortgage, these loans had the same or higher incidence of default as a loan with an LTV of >90%.
***** = Since loans may have more than one characteristic, they may appear in more than one category. Totals are not adjusted to take this into account.

The claim that the GSEs loosened their underwriting standards in order to compete specifically with Wall Street can be easily dismissed—unless the Commission majority and others who have made this statement are including Countrywide (which was based in California) or other subprime lenders in the term "Wall Street." Assuming, however, that the Commission majority and other commentators have been using the term "Wall Street" to apply to the commercial and investment banks that operate in the financial markets of New York, the data show that Wall Street was not a significant participant in the subprime PMBS market between 2004 and 2007 or at any time before or after those dates. The top five players in 2004 were subprime lenders Ameriquest ($55 billion) and Countrywide ($40 billion), followed by Lehman Brothers ($27 billion), GMAC RFC ($26 billion), and New Century ($22 billion). Other than Lehman, some other Wall Street firms were scattered through the list of the top twenty-five, but were not significant players as a group.

In 2005, the biggest year for subprime issuances, the five leaders were the same, and the total for all Wall Street institutions was $137 billion, or about 27 percent of the $508 billion issued that year.[44] In 2006, Lehman had dropped out of the top five and Countrywide

---

44. Inside Mortgage Finance, *The 2009 Mortgage Market Statistical Annual—Volume II,* pp. 139 and 140.

had taken over the leadership among the issuers, but Wall Street's share had not significantly changed. By the middle of 2007, the PMBS market had declined to such a degree that the market share numbers were meaningless. However, in that year, the GSEs' market share in NTMs increased because they had to continue buying NTMs—even though others had defaulted or left the business—in order to comply with the AH goals. Accordingly, if Fannie had ever loosened its lending standards to compete with some group, that group was not Wall Street.

The next question is whether the GSEs loosened their underwriting standards to compete with Countrywide, Ameriquest, and the other subprime lenders who were the dominant players in the PMBS market between 2004 and 2007. Again, the answer seems clearly to be no. The subprime PMBS market was very small until 2002, when for the first time it exceeded $100 billion and reached $134 billion in subprime PMBS issuances.[45] Yet, table 7 shows that in 2002 alone, the GSEs bought $206 billion in subprime loans, more than the total amount securitized by all the subprime lenders and others combined in that year.

The discussion of internal documents that follows will focus almost exclusively on Fannie Mae. The Commission concentrated its investigation on Fannie, and it was from Fannie that the Commission received the most complete set of internal documents.

By the early 2000s, Countrywide had succeeded in creating an integrated system of mortgage distribution that included originating, packaging, issuing, and underwriting NTMs through PMBS. Other subprime lenders, as noted above, were also major issuers, but they sold their PMBS through Wall Street firms that were functioning as underwriters.

The success of Countrywide and other subprime lenders as distributors of NTMs through PMBS was troubling to Fannie for two reasons. First, Countrywide had been Fannie's largest supplier of subprime mortgages; the fact that it could now securitize mortgages it formerly sold to Fannie meant that Fannie would have more difficulty finding subprime mortgages that were AH goals-eligible. In addition, the GSEs knew that their support in Congress depended heavily on meeting the AH goals and "leading the market" in lending to low-income borrowers. In 2005 and 2006, the Bush administration and a growing number of Republicans in Congress were calling for tighter regulation of Fannie and Freddie, and the GSEs needed allies in Congress to hold this off. The fact that subprime lenders were taking an increasing market share in these years—suggesting that the GSEs were no longer the most important sources of low-income mortgage credit—was thus a matter of great concern to Fannie's management. Without strong support among the Democrats in Congress, there was a significant chance that the Republican Congress would enact tougher regulatory legislation. This was expressed at Fannie as concern about a loss of "relevance," and provoked wide-ranging consideration within the firm about how it could regain its leadership role in low-income lending.

Nevertheless, although Fannie had strong reasons for wanting to compete for market share with Countrywide and others, it did not have either the operational or financial capacity to do so. In the end, Fannie was ultimately unable to take any significant action that would regain market share from the subprime lenders or anyone else during the key

---

45. Inside Mortgage Finance, *The 2009 Market Statistical Annual—Volume II*, p. 143.

years 2005 and 2006. In the end, they reduced their underwriting standards to the degree necessary to keep pace with the increasing AH goals, but not to go significantly beyond those requirements.

In a key memo dated June 27, 2005 (the "Crossroads" memo), Tom Lund, Executive Vice President for Single Family Business, addressed the question of Fannie's loss of market share and how this share position could be regained. The date of this memo is important. It shows that even in the middle of 2005, there was still a debate going on within Fannie about *whether* to compete for market share with Countrywide and the other subprime issuers. No such competition had actually begun. Lund starts the discussion in the memo by saying: "We are at a strategic crossroad . . . [his ellipses] We face two stark choices: 1. Stay the Course [or] 2. Meet the Market Where the Market Is." "Staying the course" meant trying to maintain the mortgage quality standards that Fannie had generally followed up to that point (except as necessary to meet HUD's AH goals). "Meeting the market" meant competing with Countrywide and others, not only by acquiring substantially *more* NTMs than the AH goals required, but also by acquiring much *riskier* mortgages than Fannie—which specialized in fixed-rate mortgages—had been buying up to that time.

These riskier potential acquisitions would have included much larger numbers of Option ARMs (involving negative amortization) and other loans involving multiple (or "layered") risks with which Fannie had no prior experience. Thus, Lund noted that to compete in this business, Fannie lacked "capabilities and infrastructure . . . knowledge . . . willingness to compete on price . . . [and] a value proposition for subprime." His conclusion was as stark as the choice: *"Realistically, we are not in a position to 'Meet the Market' today."* "Therefore," Lund continued, *"we recommend that we: Pursue a 'Stay the Course' strategy and test whether market changes are cyclical vs secular."*[46] [emphasis supplied]

In the balance of the Crossroads memo, Lund notes that subprime and Alt-A loans are driving the "leakage" of "goals-rich" products to PMBS issuers. He points out the severity of the loss of market share, but never suggests that this changes his view that Fannie was unequipped to compete with Countrywide and others at that time. According to an internal FCIC staff investigation, dated March 31, 2010, other senior officials—Robert Levin (Executive Vice President and Chief Business Officer), Kenneth Bacon (Executive Vice President for Housing and Community Development), and Pamela Johnson (Senior Vice President for Single Family Business)—all concurred that Fannie should follow Lund's recommendation to "stay the course."

There is no indication in any of Fannie's documents after June 2005 that Lund's "Stay the Course" recommendation was ever changed or challenged during 2005 or 2006—the period when Fannie and Freddie were supposed to have begun to acquire large numbers of NTMs (beyond what was required to meet the AH goals) in order to compete with Countrywide or (in some tellings) Wall Street.

Thus, in June 2006, one year after the Lund Crossroads memo, Stephen B. Ashley, then the chairman of the board, told Fannie's senior executives: "2006 is a transition year. To be sure, there are still issues to resolve. The consent order with OFHEO [among other

---

46. Tom Lund, "Single Family Guarantee Business: Facing Strategic Crossroads" June 27, 2005.

TABLE 8
FANNIE MAE FINANCIAL HIGHLIGHTS

Earnings Performance:	2003	2004	2005	2006	2007
Net Income ($ billions)	8.1	5.0	6.3	4.2	−2.1
Net Interest Income ($ billions)	19.5	18.1	11.5	6.8	4.6
Guarantee Fees ($ billions)	3.4	3.8	4.0	4.3	5.1
Net Interest margin (%)	2.12	1.86	1.31	0.85	0.57
Average Guarantee Fee (bps)	21.9	21.8	22.3	22.2	23.7
Return on Common Equity (%)	27.6	16.6	19.5	11.3	−8.3
Dividend Payout Ratio (%)	20.8	42.1	17.2	32.4	N/M

things, the order raised capital requirements temporarily] is demanding. And from a strategy standpoint, *it is clear that until we have eliminated operations and control weaknesses, taking on more risk or opening new lines of business will be viewed dimly by our regulators.*"[47] [emphasis supplied] So, again, we have confirmation that Fannie's top officials did not believe that the firm was in any position—in the middle of 2006—to take on the additional risk that would be necessary to compete with Countrywide and other subprime lenders that were selling PMBS backed by subprime and other NTMs.

Moreover, there is very strong financially based evidence that Fannie either never tried or was never financially able to compete for market share with Countrywide and other subprime lenders from 2004 to 2007. For example, set out in table 8 are Fannie's key financial data, published by OFHEO, its former regulator, in early 2008.[48]

Table 8 shows that Fannie's average guarantee fee *increased* during the period from 2003 to 2007. To understand the significance of this, it is necessary to understand the way the mortgage business works. Most of Fannie's guarantee business—the business that competed with securitizations of PMBS by Countrywide and others—was done with wholesale sellers of mortgage pools. In these deals, the wholesaler or issuer, a Countrywide or a Wells Fargo, would assemble a pool of mortgages and look for a guarantee mechanism that would offer the best pricing. In the case of a Fannie MBS, the key issue was the GSEs' guarantee fee, because that determined how much of the profit the issuer would be able to retain. In the case of a PMBS issue, it was the amount and cost of the credit enhancement needed to attain a AAA rating for a large percentage of the securities backed by the mortgage pool.

The issuer had a choice of securitizing through Fannie, Freddie, or one of the Wall Street underwriters. Thus, if Fannie wanted to compete with the private issuers for subprime and other loans, there was only one way to do it—by reducing its guarantee fees (called "G-fees" at Fannie and Freddie) and in this way making itself a more attractive outlet than using a Wall Street underwriter. The fact that Fannie does not appear to have done so is strong evidence that it never tried to compete for share with Countrywide and the other subprime issuers after the date of the Crossroads memo in June 2005.

---

47. Stephen B. Ashley, Fannie Mae Chairman, remarks at senior management meeting, June 27, 2006.
48. OFHEO, "Mortgage Markets and the Enterprises in 2007," pp. 33–34.

TABLE 9
FANNIE MAE'S ACQUISITION OF SUBPRIME LOANS, 2004–2007

	2004	2005	2006	2007
FICO <620	5%	5%	6%	6%
FICO 620–<660	11%	11%	11%	12%

SOURCES: Fannie's 2004 10-K. These totals do not include Fannie's purchases of subprime PMBS.
http://www.fanniemae.com/ir/pdf/sec/2004/2004_form10K.pdf;jsessionid=N3RRJCZPD5SOVJ2FQSHSFGI, p.141 and
Fannie's 2007 10-K, http://www.fanniemae.com/ir/pdf/sec/2008/form10k_022708.pdf;jsessionid=N3RRJCZPD5SOVJ2FQS
HSFGI, p. 127.

The OFHEO financial summary also shows that Fannie, in reality, had very little flexibility to compete by lowering its G-fees. Its net income and its return on equity were all declining quickly during this period, and a cut in its G-fees would have hastened this decline.

Finally, there are Fannie's own reports about its acquisitions of subprime loans. According to Fannie's 10-K reports for 2004 (which, as restated, covered periods through 2006) and 2007, Fannie's acquisition of subprime loans barely increased from 2004 through 2007. The numbers are shown in table 9.

These percentages are consistent with Fannie's effort to comply with the gradual increase in the AH goals during the years 2004 through 2007; they are not consistent with an effort to substantially increase its purchases of subprime mortgages in order to compete with firms like Countrywide that were growing their market share through securitizing subprime and other loans.

Finally, Fannie's 2005 10-K (which, as restated and filed in May 2007, also covered 2005 and 2006), contains a statement similar to that made in 2006, confirming that the GSE made no effort to compete for subprime loans (except as necessary to meet the AH goals), and that, in fact, it lost market share by declining to do so in 2004, 2005, and 2006:

> [I]n recent years, an increasing proportion of single-family mortgage loan originations has consisted of non-traditional mortgages such as interest-only mortgages, negative-amortizing mortgages and sub-prime mortgages, and demand for traditional 30-year fixed-rate mortgages has decreased. *We did not participate in large amounts of these non-traditional mortgages in 2004, 2005 and 2006* because we determined that the pricing offered for these mortgages often offered insufficient compensation for the additional credit risk associated with these mortgages. *These trends and our decision not to participate in large amounts of these non-traditional mortgages contributed to a significant loss in our share of new single-family mortgages-related securities issuances to private-label issuers during this period, with our market share decreasing from 45.0% in 2003 to 29.2% in 2004, 23.5% in 2005 and 23.7 in 2006.*[49] [emphasis supplied]

Accordingly, despite losing market share to Countrywide and others in 2004, 2005, and 2006, Fannie did not attempt to acquire unusual numbers of subprime loans in order to

---

49. Fannie Mae, 2005 10-K, p. 37.

regain this share. Instead, it continued to acquire only the subprime and other NTM loans that were necessary to meet the AH goals. That the AH goals were Fannie's sole motive for acquiring NTMs is shown by the firm's actions after the PMBS market collapsed in 2007. At that point, Fannie's market share began to rise as Countrywide and others could not continue to issue PMBS. Nevertheless, despite the losses on subprime loans that were beginning to show up in the markets, Fannie continued to buy NTMs until they were taken over by the government in September 2008. The reason for this nearly reckless behavior is obvious—they were still subject to the AH goals, which were increasing through this period. If they had only acquired these NTMs to compete with Countrywide and others for market share, the competition was already over; their competitors had abandoned the field. But the fact is that Fannie did not—or could not—increase its market share between 2004 and 2006 shows without question that market share was not the reason they had acquired so many NTMs by the time they failed in September 2008.

Beleaguered by accounting problems, suffering diminished profitability, and lacking the capability to evaluate the risks of the new kinds of mortgages they would have to buy, Fannie had no option but to stay the course it had been following for fifteen years. The NTMs they bought during the period from 2004 to 2007 were acquired to comply with the AH goals and not to increase their market share—as much as Fannie might have preferred to do so. Fannie's market share finally did increase in 2007, when the asset-backed market collapsed, Countrywide weakened, and neither Countrywide nor anyone else could continue to securitize mortgages. In a report to the board of directors on October 16, 2007, Mudd reported that Fannie's market share, which was 20 percent of the whole market at the beginning of 2007, had risen to 42 percent.[50]

That leaves one other possibility—that Fannie and Freddie were buying NTMs because they were profitable. That issue is addressed in the next section.

Did Fannie Acquire NTMs Because These Loans Were Profitable?

From time to time, commentators on the GSEs have suggested that the GSEs' real motive for acquiring NTMs was not that they had to comply with the AH goals, but that they were seeking the profits these risky loans produced. This could have been true in the 1990s, but after the major increase in the AH goals in 2000, Fannie began to recognize that complying with the goals was reducing the firm's profitability. By 2007, Fannie was asking for relief from the goals.

Table 10, drawn from a FHFA publication, shows the applicable AH goals over the period from 1996 through 2008 and the GSEs' success in meeting them.

As the table shows, Fannie and Freddie exceeded the AH goals virtually each year, but not by significant margins. They simply kept pace with the increases in the goals as these requirements came into force over the years. This alone suggests that they did not increase their purchases in order to earn profits. If that was their purpose, they would have substantially exceeded the goals, since their financial advantages (low financing costs and low

---

50. Fannie Mae, Minutes of a Meeting of the Board of Directors, October 16, 2007, p. 18.

TABLE 10
GSEs' SUCCESS IN MEETING AFFORDABLE HOUSING GOALS, 1996–2008

	1996	1997	1998	1999	2000	2001	2002	2003	2004	2005	2006	2007	2008
Low & Mod Housing Goals	40%	42%	42%	42%	42%	50%	50%	50%	50%	52%	53%	55%	56%
Fannie Actual	45%	45%	44%	46%	50%	51%	52%	52%	53%	55%	57%	56%	54%
Freddie Actual	41%	43%	43%	46%	50%	53%	50%	51%	52%	54%	56%	56%	51%
Special Affordable Goal	12%	14%	14%	14%	14%	20%	20%	20%	20%	22%	23%	25%	27%
Fannie Actual	15%	17%	15%	18%	19%	22%	21%	21%	24%	24%	28%	27%	26%
Freddie Actual	14%	15%	16%	18%	21%	23%	20%	21%	23%	26%	26%	26%	23%
Underserved Goal	21%	24%	24%	24%	24%	31%	31%	31%	31%	37%	38%	38%	39%
Fannie Actual	25%	29%	27%	27%	31%	33%	33%	32%	32%	41%	43%	43%	39%
Freddie Actual	28%	26%	26%	27%	29%	32%	31%	33%	34%	43%	44%	43%	38%

SOURCE: FHFA Mortgage Market Note 10-2, http://www.fhfa.gov/webfiles/15408/Housing%20Goals%201996-2009%20
02-01.pdf.pdf.

capital requirements) allowed them to pay more for the mortgages they wanted than any of their competitors. As HUD noted in 2000: "Because the GSEs have a funding advantage over other market participants, they have the ability to underprice their competitors and increase their market share."[51]

As early as 1999, there were clear concerns at Fannie about how the 50 percent LMI goal—which HUD had signaled as its next move—would be met. In a June 15, 1999, memorandum,[52] four Fannie staff members proposed three categories of rules changes that would enable Fannie to meet the goals more easily: (i) persuade HUD to change the goals accounting (what goes into the numerator and denominator); (ii) enter other businesses where the pickings might be goals-rich, such as manufactured housing and, significantly, Alt-A and subprime ("Efforts to expand into Alt-A and A-markets [the highest grade of subprime lending] should also yield incremental business that will have a salutary effect on our low- and moderate-income score"); and (iii) persuade HUD to adopt different methods of goals scoring.

By 2000, Fannie was effectively in competition with banks that were required to make mortgage loans under CRA to roughly the same population of low-income borrowers targeted in HUD's AH goals. Rather than selling their CRA loans to Fannie and Freddie, banks and S&Ls had begun to retain the loans in portfolio. In a presentation in November 2000, Barry Zigas, a Senior Vice President of Fannie, noted: "Our own anecdotal evidence suggests that this increase [in banks' and S&Ls' holding loans in portfolio] is due in part to below-market CRA products."[53] In other words, banks and S&Ls subject to CRA were making mortgage loans at below-market interest rates, and thus could not sell them without taking losses. This was troubling for Fannie because it meant that in order to capture these

51. http://frwebgate.access.gpo.gov/cgi-bin/getdoc.cgi?dbname=2000_register&docid=page+65093-65142.

52. Bell, Kinney, Kunde, and Weech, through Zigas and Marks internal memo to Frank Raines, "RE: HUD Housing Goals Options," June 15, 1999.

53. Barry Zigas, "Fannie Mae and Minority Lending: Assessment and Action Plan," Presentation, November 16, 2000.

loans, they would have to increase what they were willing to pay for the loans. Doing so would underprice the risks they would be assuming.

It is important to recognize what was happening. Fannie, and the banks and S&Ls under CRA, were now competing for the same kinds of NTMs, and were doing so by lowering their mortgage underwriting standards and adding flexibilities and subsidies. Simply as a result of supply and demand, all of the participants in this competition were required to pay higher prices for these increasingly risky mortgages. The banks and S&Ls that acquired these loans could not sell them without taking a loss when market interest rates were higher than the rates on the mortgages. This is the first indication in the documents that the FCIC received from Fannie that competition for subprime loans among the GSEs, banks, S&Ls, and FHA was causing the underpricing of risk—one of the principal causes of the mortgage meltdown and thus the financial crisis.

In January 2003, Fannie began planning for how to confront HUD before the next round of increases in the AH goals, expected to occur in 2004. In an "Action Plan for the Housing Goals Rewrite," dated January 22, 2003, Fannie staff reviewed a number of options, and concluded that "Fannie should strongly oppose: goals increases and new subgoals" (Slide 35).[54]

In March 2003, as Fannie prepared for new increases in the AH goals, its staff prepared a presentation, perhaps for HUD or for policy defense in public forums. The apparent purpose was to show that the goals should not be increased significantly in 2004. Slide 5 stated:

> In 2002, Fannie Mae exceeded all our goals for the 9th straight year. But it was probably the most challenging environment we've ever faced. Meeting the goals required heroic 4th quarter efforts on the part of many across the company. Vacations were cancelled. The midnight oil burned. Moreover, the challenge freaked out the business side of the house. Especially because the tenseness around meeting the goals meant that we considered not doing deals—not fulfilling our liquidity function—*and did deals at risks and prices we would not have otherwise done.*[55] [emphasis supplied]

By September 2004, it was becoming clear that continuing increases in the AH goals were having a major adverse effect on Fannie's profitability. In a memorandum to Brian Graham (another Fannie official), Paul Weech, Director of Market Research and Policy Development, wrote: "Meeting the goals in difficult markets imposes significant costs on the Company and potentially causes market-distorting behaviors. In 1998, 2002, and 2003 especially, the Company has had to pursue certain transactions as much for housing goals attainment as for the economics of the transaction."[56]

In a June 2005 presentation entitled "Costs and Benefits of Mission Activities,"[57] the authors noted in slide 10 that AH goal costs had risen from $2,632,500 in 2000 to $13,447,500 in 2003. Slide 17 is entitled "Meeting Future HUD Goals Appear Quite Daunting and Potentially Costly" and reports: "Based on 2003 experience where goal acquisition

54. Fannie Mae, "Action Plan for the Housing Goals Rewrite," January 22, 2003.
55. Fannie Mae, "The HUD Housing Goals," March 2003.
56. Fannie Mae, internal memo, Paul Weech to Brian Graham, "RE: Mission Legislation," September 3, 2004.
57. Fannie Mae, "Costs and Benefits of Mission Activities, Project Phineas," June 14, 2005.

costs (relative to Fannie Mae model fees) cost between $65 per goals unit in the first quarter to $370 per unit in the fourth quarter, meeting the shortfall could cost the company $6.5–$36.5 million to purchase sufficient units." The presentation concludes (slide 20): "Cost of mission activities—explicit and implicit—over the 2000–2004 period likely averaged approximately $200 million per year."

Earlier, I noted the efforts of Fannie and Freddie to window-dress their records for HUD by temporarily acquiring loans that would comply with the AH goals, while giving the seller the option to reacquire the loans at a later time. In 2005, we begin to see efforts by Fannie's staff to accomplish the same window-dressing in another way—delaying acquisitions of non-goal-eligible loans so that Fannie could meet the AH goals in that year; we also see the first efforts to calculate systematically the effect of goal-compliance on Fannie's profitability. In a presentation dated September 30, 2005, Barry Zigas, the key Fannie official on affordable housing, outlined a "business deferral option." Under that initiative, Fannie would ask seven major lenders to defer until 2006 sending non-goal loans to Fannie for acquisition. This would reduce the denominator of the AH goal computation and thus bring Fannie nearer to goal compliance in the fourth quarter of 2005. The cost of the deferral alone was estimated at $30–$38 million.[58]

In a presentation to HUD on October 31, 2005, entitled "Update on Fannie Mae's Housing Goals Performance,"[59] Fannie noted several "Undesirable Tradeoffs Necessary to Meet Goals." These included significant additional credit risk, and negative returns ("Deal economics are well below target returns; some deals are producing negative returns" and "G-fees may not cover expected losses"). One of the most noteworthy points was the following: "Liquidity to Questionable Products: Buying exotic product encourages continuation of risky lending; many products present with significant risk-layering; consumers are at risk of payment shock and loss of equity; potential need to waive our responsible lending policies to get goals business."

Much of the narrative about the financial crisis posits that unscrupulous and unregulated mortgage originators tricked borrowers into taking on bad mortgages. The idea that predatory lending was a major source of the NTMs in the financial system in 2008 is a significant element of the Commission majority's report, although the Commission was never able to provide any data to support this point. This Fannie slide suggests that loans later dubbed "predatory" might actually have been made to comply with the AH goals. This possibility is suggested, too, in a message sent in 2004 to Freddie's CEO, Richard Syron, by Freddie's chief risk manager, David Andrukonis, when Syron was considering whether to authorize a "Ninja" (no income/no jobs/no assets) product that he ultimately approved. Andrukonis argued against authorizing Freddie's purchase: "The potential for the perception and reality of predatory lending, with this product is great."[60] But the product was

58. Barry Zigas, "Housing Goals and Minority Lending," September 30, 2005.

59. Fannie Mae, "Update on Fannie Mae's Housing Goals Performance," Presentation to the U.S. Department of Housing and Development, October 31, 2005.

60. Freddie Mac, internal email, Donna Cogswell on behalf of David Andrukonis to Dick Syron, "RE: No Income/No Asset (NINA) Mortgages," September 7, 2004.

TABLE 11
FANNIE MAE TOOK LOSSES ON HIGHER-RISK MORTGAGES
NECESSARY TO MEET THE AFFORDABLE HOUSING GOALS

Individual Enhancements (cost analysis for "base" MCM enhancement-not layered)	30 YR FRM		
	Model Fee	Average Default %	Gap
Base: 100% LTV, 20% MI	106	34	−68.50
Interest First (IF)	129	40	−91.50
Seller Contribution (SC)	115	23	−77.50
Temporary B/D (BD)	118	37	−80.50
Zero Down (ZD)	106	34	−68.50
Manufactured Housing (MH)	227	42	−189.50

SOURCE: Memo from Rumfola, Parsons, and Kim (Single Family Business Product Management and Development) to Single Family Business Credit Committee, May 5, 2006, p.6 (FM-FCIC_00171986).

approved by Freddie, probably for the reason stated by another Freddie employee: "The Alt-A [(low doc/no doc)] business makes a contribution to our HUD goals."[61]

On May 5, 2006, a Fannie staff memo to the Single Family Business Credit Committee revealed the serious credit and financial problems Fannie was facing when acquiring subprime mortgages to meet the AH goals. The memo describes the competitive landscape, in which "product enhancements from Freddie Mac, FHA, Alt-A and subprime lenders have all contributed to increased competition for goals rich loans. . . . On the issue of seller contributions [in which the seller of the home pays cash expenses for the buyer] even FHA has expanded their guidelines by allowing 6% contributions for LTVs up to 97% that can be used toward closing, prepaid expenses, discount points and other financing concessions."[62]

The memorandum is eye-opening for what it says about the credit risks Fannie had to take in order to get the goals-rich loans it needed to meet HUD's AH requirements for 2006. Table 11 shows the costs of NTMs in terms of the G-fee "gap." (In order to determine whether a loan contributed to a return on equity, Fannie used a G-fee pricing model that took into account credit risk as well as a number of other factors; a G-fee "gap" was the difference between the G-fees required by the pricing model for a particular loan to contribute to a return on equity and a loan that did not.) The table in this memo shows the results for three subprime products under consideration, a thirty-year fixed-rate mortgage (FRM), a five-year ARM, and thirty-five- and forty-year fixed-rate mortgages. For simplicity, this analysis will discuss only the thirty-year fixed-rate product. The table shows that the base product, the thirty-year FRM, with *a zero* downpayment should be priced according to the model at a G-fee of 106 basis points. However, the memo reports that Fannie is actually buying loans like that at a price consistent with an annual fee of 37.50 bps, producing a gap (or loss from the model) of 68.50 bps. The reason the gap is so large is shown in the table: the

61. Freddie Mac, internal email from Mike May to Dick Syron, "FW: FINAL NINA Memo," October 6, 2004.

62. FCIC, internal memo, Single Family Business Product Management and Development to Single Family Business Credit Committee, "RE: PMD Proposal for Increasing Housing Goal Loans," May 5, 2006, p. 6.

anticipated default rate on that zero-down mortgage was *34 percent*. The table then goes on to consider other possible loan alternatives, all of which produce disastrous consequences:

From this report, it is clear that in order to meet the AH goals, Fannie had to pay up for goals-rich mortgages, taking a huge credit risk along the way.

The dismal financial results that were developing at Fannie as a result of the AH goals were also described in Fannie's 10-K report for 2006, which anticipated both losses of revenue and higher credit losses as a result of acquiring the mortgages required by the AH goals:

> [W]e have made, and continue to make, significant adjustments to our mortgage loan sourcing and purchase strategies in an effort to meet HUD's increased housing goals and new subgoals. These strategies include entering into some purchase and securitization transactions with *lower expected economic returns than our typical transactions*. We have also relaxed some of our underwriting criteria to obtain goals-qualifying mortgage loans and increased our investments in higher-risk mortgage loan products that are more likely to serve the borrowers targeted by HUD's goals and subgoals, *which could increase our credit losses.*[63] [emphasis supplied]

The underlying reasons for the "lower expected returns" were reported in February 2007 in a document the FCIC received from Fannie, which noted that for 2006 the "cash flow cost" of meeting the housing goals was $140 million, while the "opportunity cost" was $470 million.[64] In a report to HUD on the AH goals, dated April 11, 2007, Fannie described these costs as follows: "The largest costs [of meeting the goals] are opportunity costs of foregone revenue. In 2006, opportunity cost was about $400 million, whereas the cash flow cost was about $134 million. If opportunity cost was $0, our shareholders would be indifferent to the deal. The cash flow cost is the implied out of pocket cost."[65]

By this time, "Alignment Meetings"—in which Fannie staff considered how they would meet the AH goals—were taking place almost monthly (according to the frequency with which presentations to Alignment meetings occur in the documentary record). In an Alignment Meeting on June 22, 2007, on a "Housing Goals Forecast," three plans were considered for meeting the 2007 AH goals, even though half the year was already gone. One of the plans was forecast to result in opportunity costs of $767.7 million, while the other two plans resulted in opportunity costs of $817.1 million.[66] In a Forecast meeting on July 27, 2007, a "Plan to Meet Base Goals," which probably meant the topline LMI goal including all subgoals, was placed at $1.156 billion for 2007.[67]

In a December 21, 2007 letter to Brian Montgomery, Assistant Secretary of Housing, Fannie CEO Daniel Mudd asked that, in light of the financial and economic conditions

---

63. Fannie Mae, 2006 10-K, p. 146.

64. Fannie Mae, "Business Update," presentation. "Cash flow cost" equals expected revenue minus expected loss. Expected revenue is what will be received in G-fees; expected loss includes G&A and credit losses. "Opportunity cost" is the G-fee actually charged minus the model fee—the fee that Fannie's model would impose to guarantee a mortgage of the same quality in order to earn a fair market return on capital.

65. Fannie Mae, "Housing Goals Briefing for HUD," April 11, 2007

66. Fannie Mae, "Housing Goals Forecast," Alignment Meeting, June 22, 2007.

67. Fannie Mae, Forecast Meeting, July 27, 2007.

then prevailing in the country—particularly the absence of a PMBS market and the increasing number of mortgage delinquencies and defaults—HUD's AH goals for 2007 be declared "infeasible." He noted that HUD also has an obligation to "consider the financial condition of the enterprise when determining the feasibility of goals." Then he continued: "Fannie Mae submits that the company took all reasonable actions to meet the subgoals that were both financially prudent and likely to contribute to the achievement of the subgoals. . . . *In 2006, Fannie Mae relaxed certain underwriting standards and purchased some higher risk mortgage loan products in an effort to meet the housing goals.* The company continued to purchase higher risk loans into 2007, and believes these efforts to acquire goals-rich loans are partially responsible for increasing credit losses."[68] [emphasis supplied]

This statement confirms two facts that are critical on the question of why Fannie (and Freddie) acquired so many high-risk loans in 2006 and earlier years: first, the companies were trying to meet the AH goals established by HUD and did not pursue these loans because they were profitable. It also shows that the efforts of HUD and others—including the Commission majority in its report—to blame the managements of Fannie and Freddie for purchasing the loans that ultimately dragged them to insolvency is misplaced.

Finally, in a July 2009 report, the Federal Housing Finance Agency (FHFA, the GSEs' new regulator, replacing OFHEO) noted that Fannie and Freddie both followed the practice of cross-subsidizing the subprime and Alt-A loans that they acquired:

> Although Fannie Mae and Freddie Mac consider model-derived estimates of cost in determining the single-family guarantee fees they charge, their pricing often subsidizes their guarantees on some mortgages using higher returns they expect to earn on guarantees of other loans. In both 2007 and 2008, cross-subsidization in single-family guarantee fees charged by the Enterprises was evident across product types, credit score categories, and LTV ratio categories. In each case, there were cross-subsidies from mortgages that posed lower credit risk on average to loans that posed higher credit risk. The greatest estimated subsidies generally went to the highest-risk mortgages.[69]

The higher-risk mortgages were the ones most needed by Fannie and Freddie to meet the AH goals. Needless to say, there is no need to cross-subsidize the G-fees of loans that are acquired because they are profitable.

Accordingly, both market share and profitability must be excluded as reasons that Fannie (and Freddie) acquired subprime and Alt-A loans between 2004 and 2007. The only remaining motive—and the valid one—was the effect of the AH goals imposed by HUD.

In 2008, after its takeover by the government, Fannie Mae finally published a credit supplement to its 2008 10-K, which contained an accounting of its subprime and Alt-A credit exposure. Table 12 is reproduced on page 78 in order to provide a picture of the kinds of loans Fannie acquired in order to meet the AH goals. Loans may appear in more than one category, so the table does not reveal Fannie's total net exposure to each category, nor does it

---

68. Fannie Mae letter, Daniel Mudd to Asst. Secretary Brian Montgomery, December 21, 2007, p. 6.
69. FHFA, Fannie Mae and Freddie Mac Single Family Guarantee Fees in 2007 and 2008, p. 33.

include Fannie's holdings of non-Fannie MBS or PMBS, for which it did not have loan-level data. Note the reference to $8.4 billion in the column for subprime loans. As noted earlier, Fannie classified as subprime only those loans that it purchased from subprime lenders. However, Fannie included loans with FICO scores of less than 660 in the table, indicating that they are not prime loans but without classifying them formally as subprime.

In a later credit supplement, filed in August 2009, Fannie eliminated the duplications among the loans in table 12, and reported that as of June 30, 2009, it held the credit risk on NTMs with a total unpaid principal amount of $2.7 trillion. The average loan amount was $151,000, for a total of 5.73 million NTM loans.[70] This number does not include Fannie's holdings of subprime PMBS as to which it did not have loan-level data.

Freddie Mac. As noted earlier, in its limited review of the role of the GSEs in the financial crisis, the Commission spent most of its time and staff resources on a review of Fannie Mae, and for that reason this dissent focuses primarily on documents received from Fannie. However, things were not substantially different at Freddie Mac. In a document dated June 4, 2009, entitled "Cost of Freddie Mac's Affordable Housing Mission," a report to the Business Risk Committee of the Board of Directors,[71] several points were made that show the experience of Freddie was no different from Fannie's:

- Our housing goals compliance required little direct subsidy prior to 2003, but since then subsidies have averaged $200 million per year.
- Higher credit risk mortgages disproportionately tend to be goal-qualifying. Targeted affordable lending generally requires "accepting" substantially higher credit risk.
- We charge more for targeted (and baseline) affordable single-family loans, but not enough to fully offset their higher incremental risk.
- Goal-qualifying single-family loans accounted for the disproportionate share of our 2008 realized losses that was predicted by our models. (Slide 2)
- In 2007 Freddie Mac failed two subgoals, but compliance was subsequently deemed infeasible by the regulator due to economic conditions. In 2008 Freddie Mac failed six goals and subgoals, five of which were deemed infeasible. No enforcement action was taken regarding the sixth missed goal because of our financial condition. (Slide 3)
- Goal-qualifying loans tend to be higher risk. Lower household income correlates with various risk factors such as less wealth, less employment stability, higher loan-to-value ratios, or lower credit scores. (Slide 7)
- Targeted affordable loans have much higher expected default probabilities. . . Over one-half of targeted affordable loans have higher expected default probabilities than the highest 5% of non-goal-qualifying loans. (Slide 8)

---

70. http://www.fanniemae.com/ir/pdf/sec/2009/q2credit_summary.pdf, p. 5.

71. Freddie Mac, "Cost of Freddie Mac's Affordable Housing Mission," Business Risk Committee, Board of Directors, June 4, 2009.

TABLE 12

FANNIE MAE CREDIT PROFILE BY KEY PRODUCT FEATURES: CREDIT CHARACTERISTICS OF SINGLE-FAMILY CONVENTIONAL MORTGAGE CREDIT BOOK OF BUSINESS

As of December 31, 2008	Overall Book	Negative-Amortizing Loans	Interest-Only Loans	Loans with FICO <620	Loans with FICO ≥ 620 and < 660	Loans with Original LTV Ratio >90%	Loans with FICO < 620 and Original LTV Ratio > 90%	Alt-A Loans[1]	Subprime Loans[1]	Jumbo Conforming Loans[1]
Unpaid Principal Balance (billions)*	$2,730.9	$17.3	$212.9	$123.0	$256.1	$278.3	$27.3	$292.4	$8.4	$19.9
Share of Single-Family Conventional Credit Book[1]	100.0%	0.6%	7.8%	4.5%	9.4%	10.2%	1.0%	10.1%	0.3%	0.7%
Average Unpaid Principal Balance	$148,824	$142,502	$241,943	$126,604	$141,746	$141,569	$119,607	$170,250	$150,445	$579,528
Serious Delinquency Rate	2.42%	5.61%	8.42%	9.03%	5.64%	6.33%	15.97%	7.03%	14.29%	0.12%
Origination Years 2005–2007	46.5%	62.0%	80.9%	56.3%	55.0%	58.8%	69.8%	72.7%	80.7%	1.4%
Weighted Average Original LTV Ratio	71.8%	71.1%	75.4%	76.7%	77.5%	97.3%	98.1%	72.6%	77.2%	68.4%
Original LTV Ratio >90	10.2%	0.3%	9.1%	22.2%	21.1%	100.0%	100.0%	5.3%	6.8%	0.0%
Weighted Average Mark-to-Market LTV Ratio	70.0%	87.2%	93.4%	76.3%	77.5%	97.6%	97.7%	81.0%	87.3%	69.9%
Mark-to-Market LTV Ratio >100	11.6%	42.8%	35.6%	15.9%	17.6%	38.2%	38.5%	23.2%	24.5%	0.4%
Weighted Average FICO	724	698	725	588	641	694	592	719	623	762
FICO < 620	4.5%	10.7%	1.3%	100.0%	0.0%	9.8%	100.0%	0.7%	47.6%	0.6%
FICO ≥ 620 and <660	9.4%	10.1%	7.7%	0.0%	100.0%	19.4%	0.0%	8.7%	27.8%	0.2%
Fixed-Rate	90.0%	0.1%	39.6%	93.6%	92.3%	94.2%	96.5%	72.3%	73.1%	95.2%
Principal Residence	89.7%	70.4%	84.9%	96.8%	94.4%	97.1%	99.4%	77.8%	96.6%	98.2%
Condo/Co-op	9.4%	13.5%	16.2%	4.9%	6.6%	9.8%	5.9%	10.8%	4.7%	11.5%
Credit Enhanced[2]	20.9%	76.3%	35.0%	35.0%	36.3%	92.5%	94.1%	38.6%	63.4%	11.3%
% of 2007 Credit Losses[3]	100.0%	0.9%	15.0%	18.8%	21.9%	17.4%	6.4%	29.2%	1.0%	0.0%
% of 2008 Q3 Credit Losses[3]	100.0 %	3.8%	36.2%	11.3%	16.8%	21.5%	5.4%	47.6%	2.1%	0.2%
% of 2008 Q4 Credit Losses[3]	100.0%	2.2%	33.1%	11.5%	17.2%	23.1%	5.2%	43.2%	2.0%	1.1%
% of 2008 Credit Losses[3]	100.0%	2.9%	34.2%	11.8%	17.4%	21.3%	5.4%	45.6%	2.0%	0.4%

SOURCE: Fannie Mae, Credit Supplement to 2008 10-K, filed February 26, 2009, p. 5.

NOTES: (1) = Alt-A, Subprime, and Jumbo Conforming Loans are calculated as a percentage of the single-family mortgage credit book of business, which includes government loans. Government loans are guaranteed or insured by the U.S. Government or its agencies, such as the Department of Veterans Affairs (VA), the Federal Housing Administration (FHA) or the Rural Housing and Community Facilities Program and the Department of Agriculture.

(2) = Unpaid principal balance of all loans with credit enhancement as a percentage of unpaid principal balance of single-family conventional mortgage credit book of business. Includes primary mortgage insurance, pool insurance, lender recourse and other credit enhancement.

(3) = Expressed as a percentage of credit losses for the single-family mortgage credit book of business. For information on total credit losses, refer to Fannie Mae's 2008 Form 10-K.

The use of the affordable housing goals to force a reduction in the GSEs' underwriting standards was a major policy error committed by HUD in two successive administrations, and must be recognized as such if we are ever to understand what caused the financial crisis. Ultimately, the AH goals extended the housing bubble, infused it with weak and high-risk NTMs, caused the insolvency of Fannie and Freddie, and—together with other elements of U.S. housing policy—was the principal cause of the financial crisis itself.

When Congress enacted the Housing and Economic Recovery Act of 2008 (HERA), it transferred the responsibility for administering the affordable housing goals from HUD to FHFA. In 2010, FHFA modified and simplified the AH goals, and eliminated one of their most troubling elements. As Fannie had noted, if the AH goals exceed the number of goals-eligible borrowers in the market, they were being forced to allocate credit, taking it from the middle class and providing it to low-income borrowers. In effect, there was a conflict between their mission to advance affordable housing and their mission to maintain a liquid secondary mortgage market for most mortgages in the United States. The new FHFA rule does not require the GSEs to purchase more qualifying loans than the percentage of the total market that these loans constitute.[72]

This does not solve all of the major problems with the AH goals. In the sense that the goals enable the government to direct where a private company extends credit, they are inherently a form of government credit allocation. More significantly, the competition among the GSEs, FHA, and the banks that are required under the CRA to find and acquire the same kind of loans will continue to cause the same underpricing of risk on these loans that eventually brought about the mortgage meltdown and the financial crisis. This is discussed in the next section and the section on the CRA.

4. COMPETITION BETWEEN THE GSES AND FHA FOR SUBPRIME AND ALT-A MORTGAGES

One of the important facts about HUD's management of the AH goals was that it placed Fannie and Freddie in direct competition with FHA, an agency within HUD. This was already noted in some of the Fannie documents cited above. Fannie treated this as a conflict of interest at HUD, but there is a strong case that this competition is exactly what HUD and Congress wanted. It is important to recall the context in which the GSE Act was enacted in 1992. In 1990, Congress had enacted the Federal Credit Reform Act.[73] One of its purposes

---

72. Federal Housing Finance Agency, 2010–2011 Enterprise Housing Goals; Enterprise Book-Entry Procedures; Final Rule, 12 CFR Parts 1249 and 1282, *Federal Register,* September 14, 2010, p. 55892.

73. Title V of the Congressional Budget Act of 1990. Under the FCRA, HUD must estimate the annual cost of FHA's credit subsidy for budget purposes. The credit subsidy is the net of its estimated receipts reduced by its estimated payments.

was to capture in the government's budget the risks to the government associated with loan guarantees, and in effect it placed a loose budgetary limit on FHA guarantees. For those in Congress and at HUD who favored increased mortgage lending to low-income borrowers and underserved communities, this consequence of the FCRA may have been troubling. What had previously been a free way to extend support to groups who were not otherwise eligible for conventional mortgages—which generally required a 20 percent downpayment and the indicia of willingness and ability to pay—now appeared to be potentially restricted. Requiring the GSEs to take up the mantle of affordable housing would have looked, at the time, like a solution, since Fannie and Freddie had unlimited access to funds in the private markets and were off-budget entities.

Looked at from this perspective, it would make sense for Congress and HUD to place the GSEs and FHA in competition, just as it made sense to put Fannie and Freddie in competition with one another for affordable loans. With all three entities competing for the same kinds of loans, and with HUD's control of both FHA's lending standards and the GSEs' affordable housing requirements, underwriting requirements would inevitably be reduced. HUD's explicit and frequently expressed interest in reducing mortgage underwriting standards, as a means of making mortgage credit available to low-income borrowers, provides ample evidence of HUD's motives for creating this competition.

Established in 1934, now a part of HUD and administered by the Federal Housing Administrator (who is also the Assistant Secretary of Housing), FHA insures 100 percent of an eligible mortgage. FHA was established to provide financing to people who could not meet the standards for a bank-originated conventional loan. The loans it insured had a maximum LTV of 80 percent in 1934. This went to 95 percent in 1950, and 97 percent in 1961.[74] With its maximum LTV remaining at 97 percent, FHA maintained average FICO scores for its borrowers just below 660 from 1996 to 2006. During this period, the average FICO score for a conventional subprime borrower was somewhat lower.[75] Beginning in 1993, shortly after Fannie and Freddie were introduced as competitors, FHA began to increase its percentage of loans with low downpayments. This had the predictable effect on its delinquency rates, as shown in figure 6, prepared by Edward Pinto with data from FHA, the FDIC, and the MBA.

Despite its reductions in required downpayments, FHA's market share vis-à-vis the GSEs began to decline. According to GAO data, in 1996, FHA's market share among lower-income borrowers was 26 percent, while the GSEs' share was 23.8 percent. By 2005, FHA's share was 9.8 percent, while the GSEs' share was 31.9 percent. It appears that early on, Fannie Mae deliberately targeted FHA borrowers with its Community Homebuyer Program (CHBP). In a memorandum prepared in 1993, Fannie's Credit Policy group compared Fannie's then-proposed CHBP program to FHA's requirements under its 1-to-4 family loan program (Section 203(b)) and showed that most of Fannie's requirements were competitive or better.

---

74. Kerry D. Vandell, "FHA Restructuring Proposals: Alternatives and Implications," *Fannie Mae Housing Policy Debate*, vol. 6, Issue 2, 1995, pp. 308–9.

75. GAO, "Federal Housing Administration: Decline in Agency's Market Share Was Associated with Product and Process Developments of Other Mortgage Market Participants," GAO-07-645, June 2007, pp. 42 and 44.

FIGURE 6

IMPACT OF FHA's INCREASING LTVs ON ANNUAL
FORECLOSURE STARTS AS A PERCENTAGE OF INSURED LOANS

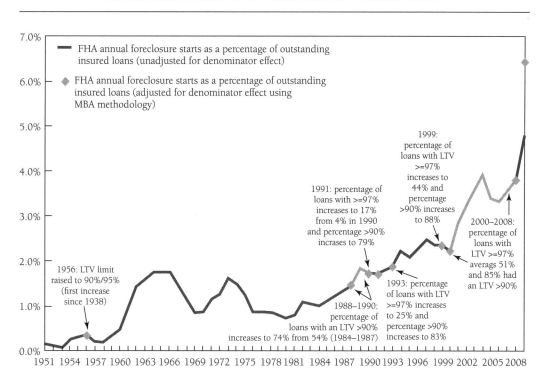

FHA also appears to have tried to lead the GSEs. In 1999—just before the AH goals for Fannie and Freddie were to be raised—FHA almost doubled its originations of loans with LTVs equal to or greater than 97 percent, going from 22.9 percent in 1998 to 43.84 percent in 1999.[76] It also offered additional concessions on underwriting standards in order to attract subprime business. The following is from a Quicken ad in January 2000 (emphasis in the original),[77] which is likely to have been based on an FHA program as it existed in 1999:

- **Borrowers can purchase with a minimum down payment.** Without FHA insurance, many families can't afford the homes they want because down payments are a major roadblock. FHA down payments range from 1.25% to 3% of the sale price and are significantly lower than the minimum that many lenders require for conventional or sub-prime loans.
- **With FHA loans, borrowers need as little as 3% of the "total funds" required.** In addition to the funds needed for the down payment, borrowers also have to

---

76. Integrated Financial Engineering, "Actuarial Review of the Federal Housing Administration Mutual Mortgage Insurance Fund (Excluding HECMs) for Fiscal Year 2009," prepared for U.S. Department of Housing and Urban Development, November 6, 2009, p. 42.

77. Quicken press release, "Quicken Loans First to Offer FHA Home Mortgages Nationally on the Internet with HUD's approval, Intuit expands home ownership nationwide, offering consumers widest variety of home loan options," January 20, 2000, http://web.intuit.com/about_intuit/press_releases/2000/01-20.html.

pay closing costs, prepaid fees for insurance and interest, as well as escrow fees which include mortgage insurance, hazard insurance, and months worth of property taxes. A FHA-insured home loan can be structured so borrowers don't pay more than 3% of the total out-of-pocket funds, including the down payment.

- **The combined total of out-of-pocket funds can be a gift or loan from family members.** FHA allows homebuyers to use gifts from family members and non-profit groups to cover their down payment and additional closing costs and fees. In fact, even a 100% gift or a personal loan from a relative is acceptable.

- **FHA's credit requirements are flexible.** Compared to credit requirements established by many lenders for other types of home loans, FHA focuses only on a borrower's last 12–24 month credit history. In addition, there is no minimum FICO score—mortgage bankers look at each application on a case-by-case basis. It is also perfectly acceptable for people with NO established credit to receive a loan with this program.

- **FHA permits borrowers to have a higher debt-to-income ratio than most insurers typically allow.** Conventional home loans allow borrowers to have 36% of their gross income attributed to their new monthly mortgage payment combined with existing debt. FHA program allows borrowers to carry 41%, and in some circumstances, even more.

It is important to remember that 1999 is the year that HUD was planning a big step-up in the AH goals for the GSEs—from 42 percent LMI to 50 percent, with even larger percentage increases in the special affordable category that would be most competitive with FHA. The last major increase in the percent of FHA's loans with LTVs equal to or greater than 97 percent had occurred in 1991, the year before the GSE Act imposed the AH goals on Fannie and Freddie, and in effect directed them to consider downpayments of 5 percent or less. In 1991, FHA's percentage of loans equal to or greater than 97 percent rose suddenly from 4.4 percent to 17.1 percent.[78] Again, FHA, under the control of HUD, appears to be offering competition to the GSEs that would lead them to reduce their underwriting standards. Since FHA is a government agency, its actions cannot be explained by a profit motive. Instead, it seems clear that FHA reduced its lending standards as part of a HUD policy to lead Fannie and Freddie in the same direction.

The result of Fannie's competition with FHA in high-LTV lending is shown in the following figure, which compares the respective shares of FHA and Fannie in the category of loans with LTVs equal to or greater than 97 percent, including Fannie loans with a combined LTV equal to or greater than 97 percent.

Whether a conscious policy of HUD or not, competition between the GSEs and FHA ensued immediately after the GSEs were given their affordable housing mission in 1992. The fact that FHA, an agency controlled by HUD, substantially increased the LTVs it would accept in 1991 (just before the GSEs were given their affordable housing mission) and

---

78. GAO, "Federal Housing Administration: Decline in Agency's Market Share Was Associated with Product and Process Developments of Other Mortgage Market Participants," GAO-07-645, June 2007, pp. 42 and 44.

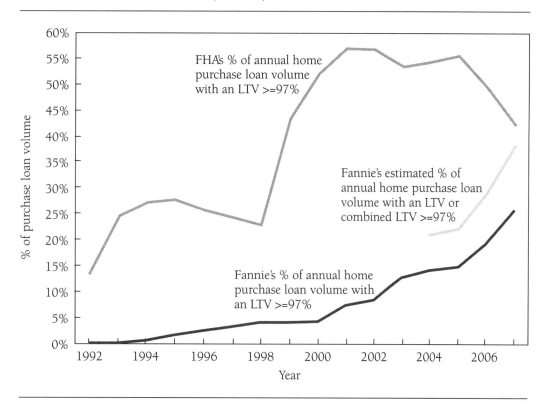

FIGURE 7
ULTRA-HIGH LTV (>=97%) LENDING BY FANNIE AND FHA

again in 1999 (just before the GSEs were required to increase their affordable housing efforts) is further evidence that HUD was coordinating these policies in the interest of creating competition between FHA and the GSEs. The effect was to drive down underwriting standards, which HUD had repeatedly described as its goal.

5. ENLISTING MORTGAGE BANKERS AND SUBPRIME LENDERS IN AFFORDABLE HOUSING

In 1994, HUD began a program to enlist other members of the mortgage financing community in the effort to reduce underwriting standards. In that year, the Mortgage Bankers Association—a group of mortgage financing firms not otherwise regulated by the federal government and not subject to HUD's legal authority—agreed to join HUD's Best Practices Initiative program.[79] The circumstances surrounding this agreement are somewhat obscure,

___

79. HUD's Best Practices Initiative was described this way by HUD: "Since 1994, HUD has signed Fair Lending Best Practices (FLBP) Agreements with lenders across the nation that are individually tailored to

but at least one contemporary account suggests that the MBA signed up to avoid an effort by HUD to cover mortgage bankers under CRA, which, up to that point, had only applied only to government-insured banks.

In mid-September 1994, the Mortgage Bankers Association of America, whose membership includes many bank-owned mortgage companies, signed a three-year master best-practices agreement with HUD. The agreement consisted of two parts: MBA's agreement to work on fair-lending issues in consultation with HUD and a model best-practices agreement that individual mortgage banks could use to devise their own agreements with HUD. The first such agreement, signed by Countrywide Funding Corp., the nation's largest mortgage bank, is summarized below. Many have seen the MBA agreement as a preemptive strike against congressional murmurings that mortgage banks should be pulled under the umbrella of the CRA.[80]

As the first member of the MBA to sign, Countrywide probably realized that there were political advantages in being seen as assisting low-income mortgage lending, and it became one of a relatively small group of subprime lenders who were to prosper enormously as Fannie and Freddie began to look for sources of the subprime loans that would enable them to meet the AH goals. By 1998, there were 117 MBA signatories to HUD's Best Practices Initiative, which was described as follows:

> The companies and associations that sign "Best Practices" Agreements not only commit to meeting the responsibilities under the Fair Housing Act, but also make a concerted effort to exceed those requirements. In general, the signatories agree to administer a review process for loan applications to ensure that all applicants have every opportunity to qualify for a mortgage. They also assent to making loans of any size so that all borrowers may be served and to provide information on all loan programs for which an applicant qualifies. . . . The results of the initiative are promising. As lenders discover new, untapped markets, their minority and low-income loans applications and originations have risen. Consequently, the homeownership rate for low-income and minority groups has increased throughout the nation.[81]

Countrywide was by far the most important participant in the HUD program. Under that program, it made a series of multi-billion-dollar commitments, culminating in a "trillion-dollar commitment" to lend to minority and low-income families, which it fulfilled in part by selling subprime and other NTMs to Fannie and Freddie. In a 2000 report, the Fannie Mae Foundation noted: "FHA loans constituted the largest share of Countrywide's

---

public-private partnerships that are considered on the leading edge. The Agreements not only offer an opportunity to increase low-income and minority lending but they incorporate fair housing and equal opportunity principles into mortgage lending standards. These banks and mortgage lenders, as represented by Countrywide Home Loans, Inc., serve as industry leaders in their communities by demonstrating a commitment to affirmatively further fair lending." Available at http://www.hud.gov/local/hi/working/nlwfal2001.cfm.

80. Steve Cocheo, "Fair-Lending Pressure Builds," *ABA Banking Journal,* vol. 86, 1994, http://www.questia.com/googleScholar.qst?docId=5001707340.

81. HUD, "Building Communities and New Markets for the 21st Century," FY 1998 Report , p. 75, http://www.huduser.org/publications/polleg/98con/NewMarkets.pdf.

activity, until Fannie Mae and Freddie Mac began accepting loans with higher LTVs and greater underwriting flexibilities."[82] In late 2007, a few months before its rescue by Bank of America, Countrywide reported that it had made $789 billion in mortgage loans toward its trillion-dollar commitment.[83]

6. THE COMMUNITY REINVESTMENT ACT

The most controversial element of the vast increase in NTMs between 1993 and 2008 was the role of the CRA.[84] The act, which is applicable only to federally insured depository institutions, was originally adopted in 1977. Its purpose, in part, was to "require each appropriate Federal financial supervisory agency to use its authority when examining financial institutions to encourage such institutions to help meet the credit needs of the local communities in which they are chartered consistent with the safe and sound operations of such institutions." The enforcement provisions of the act authorized the bank regulators to withhold approvals for such transactions as mergers and acquisitions and branch network expansion if the applying bank did not have a satisfactory CRA rating.

CRA did not have a substantial effect on subprime lending in the years after its enactment until the regulations under the act were tightened in 1995. The 1995 regulations required insured banks to acquire or make "flexible and innovative" mortgages that they would not otherwise have made. In this sense, the CRA and Fannie and Freddie's AH goals are cut from the same cloth.

There were two very distinct applications of the CRA. The first, and the one with the broadest applicability, is a requirement that all insured banks make CRA loans in their respective assessment areas. When the act is defended, it is almost always discussed in terms of this category—loans in bank assessment areas. Banks complain (usually privately) that they are required by the regulators to make imprudent loans to comply with CRA. One example is the following statement by a local community bank in a report to its shareholders:

> Under the umbrella of the Community Reinvestment Act (CRA), a tremendous amount of pressure was put on banks by the regulatory authorities to make loans, especially mortgage loans, to low income borrowers and neighborhoods. The regulators were very heavy handed regarding this issue. I will not dwell on it here but

82. Fannie Mae Foundation, "Making New Markets: Case Study of Countrywide Home Loans," 2000, http://content.knowledgeplex.org/kp2/programs/pdf/rep_newmortmkts_countrywide.pdf.

83. "Questions and Answers from Countrywide about Lending," December 11, 2007, available at http://www.realtown.com/articles/article/print/id/768.

84. 12 U.S.C. 2901.

they required [redacted name] to change its mortgage lending practices to meet certain CRA goals, even though we argued the changes were risky and imprudent.[85]

On the other hand, the regulators defend the act and their actions under it, and particularly any claim that the CRA had a role in the financial crisis. The most frequently cited defense is a speech by former Fed Governor Randall Kroszner on December 3, 2008,[86] in which he said in pertinent part:

> Only 6 percent of all the *higher-priced loans* [those that were considered CRA loans because they bore high interest rates associated with their riskier character] were extended by *CRA-covered lenders to lower-income borrowers or neighborhoods in their assessment areas*, the local geographies that are the primary focus for CRA evaluation purposes. This result undermines the assertion by critics of the potential for a substantial role for the CRA in the subprime crisis. [emphasis supplied]

There are two points in this statement that require elaboration. First, it assumes that all CRA loans are high-priced loans. This is incorrect. Many banks, in order to be sure of obtaining the necessary number of loans to attain a satisfactory CRA rating, subsidized the loans by making them at lower interest rates than their risk characteristics would warrant. This is true, in part, because CRA loans are generally loans to low-income individuals; as such, they are more likely than loans to middle-income borrowers to be subprime and Alt-A loans and thus sought after by FHA, Fannie and Freddie, and subprime lenders such as Countrywide; this competition is another reason why their rates are likely to be lower than their risk characteristics. Second, while bank lending under CRA in their assessment areas has probably not had a major effect on the overall presence of subprime loans in the U.S. financial system, it is not the element about CRA that raises the concerns about how CRA operated to increase the presence of NTMs in the housing bubble and in the U.S. financial system generally. There is another route through which CRA's role in the financial crisis is likely to be considerably more significant.

In 1994, the Riegle-Neal Interstate Banking and Branching Efficiency Act for the first time allowed banks to merge across state lines under federal law (as distinct from interstate compacts). Under these circumstances, the enforcement provisions of the CRA, which required regulators to withhold approvals of applications for banks that did not have satisfactory CRA ratings, became particularly relevant for large banks that applied to federal bank regulators for merger approvals. In a 2007 speech, Fed Chairman Ben Bernanke stated that after the enactment of the Riegle-Neal legislation, "as public scrutiny of bank merger and acquisition activity escalated, advocacy groups increasingly used the public comment process to protest bank applications on CRA grounds. In instances of highly contested applications, the Federal Reserve Board and other agencies held public meetings to allow the public and the applicants to comment on the lending records of the banks in question. In response to these new pressures, banks began to devote more resources to their CRA

---

85. Original letter in author's files.
86. Randall Kroszner, Speech at the Confronting Concentrated Poverty Forum, December 3, 2008.

programs."[87] This modest description, although accurate as far as it goes, does not fully describe the effect of the law and the application process on bank lending practices.

In 2007, the umbrella organization for many low-income or community "advocacy groups," the National Community Reinvestment Coalition, published a report entitled "CRA Commitments," which recounted the substantial success of its members in using the leverage provided by the bank application process to obtain trillions of dollars in CRA lending commitments from banks that had applied to federal regulators for merger approvals. The opening section of the report states (bolded language in the original):[88]

> **Since the passage of CRA in 1977, lenders and community organizations have signed over 446 CRA agreements totaling more than $4.5 trillion in reinvestment dollars flowing to minority and lower income neighborhoods.**
>
> Lenders and community groups will often sign these agreements when a lender has submitted an application to merge with another institution or expand its services. Lenders must seek the approval of federal regulators for their plans to merge or change their services. The four federal financial institution regulatory agencies will scrutinize the CRA records of lenders and will assess the likely future community reinvestment performance of lenders. *The application process, therefore, provides an incentive for lenders to sign CRA agreements with community groups that will improve their CRA performance. Recognizing the important role of collaboration between lenders and community groups, the federal agencies have established mechanisms in their application procedures that encourage dialogue and cooperation among the parties in preserving and strengthening community reinvestment.* [emphasis supplied]

A footnote to this statement reports:

> The Federal Reserve Board will grant an extension of the public comment period during its merger application process upon a joint request by a bank and community group. In its commentary to Regulation Y, the Board indicates that this procedure was added to facilitate discussions between banks and community groups regarding programs that help serve the convenience and needs of the community. In its Corporate Manual, the Office of the Comptroller of the Currency states that it will not offer the expedited application process to a lender that does not intend to honor a CRA agreement made by the institution that it is acquiring.

In its report, the NCRC listed all 446 commitments and includes a summary list of year-by-year commitments (see table 13):

The size of these commitments, which far outstrip the CRA loans made in assessment areas, suggests the potential significance of the CRA as a cause of the financial crisis. It is noteworthy that the Commission majority was not willing even to consider the significance

---

87. Ben S. Bernanke, "The Community Reinvestment Act: Its Evolution and New Challenges," March 30, 2007, p. 2.

88. See note 9, part I.

TABLE 13
NCRC SUMMARY LIST OF YEAR-BY-YEAR COMMITMENTS, 1977–2007

Year	Annual Dollars ($ millions)	Total Dollars ($ millions)
2007	12, 500	4,566,480
2006	258,000	4,553,980
2005	100,276	4,298,980
2004	1,631,140	4,195,704
2003	711,669	2,564,564
2002	152,859	1,852,895
2001	414,184	1,700,036
2000	13,681	1,285,852
1999	103,036	1,272,171
1998	812,160	1,169,135
1997	221,345	356,975
1996	49,678	135,630
1995	26,590	85,952
1994	6,128	59,362
1993	10,716	53,234
1992	33,708	42,518
1991	2,443	8,811
1990	1,614	6,378
1989	2,260	4,764
1988	1,248	2,504
1987	357	1,256
1986	516	899
1985	73	382
1984	219	309
1983	1	90
1982	6	89
1981	5	83
1980	13	78
1979	15	65
1978	0	50
1977	50	50

of the NCRC's numbers. In connection with its only hearing on the housing issue, and before any research had been done on the NCRC statements, the Commission published a report absolving CRA of any responsibility for the financial crisis.[89]

To understand CRA's role in the financial crisis, the relevant statistic is the $4.5 trillion in bank CRA lending commitments that the NCRC cited in its 2007 report. (This document and others that are relevant to this discussion were removed from the NCRC website,

89. FCIC, "The Community Reinvestment Act and the Mortgage Crisis," Preliminary Staff Report, http://www.fcic.gov/reports/pdfs/2010-0407-Preliminary_Staff_Report_-_CRA_and_the_Mortgage_Crisis.pdf.

www.ncrc.org, after they received publicity, but can still be found on the web).[90] One important question is whether the bank regulators cooperated with community groups by withholding approvals of applications for mergers and acquisitions until an agreement or commitment for CRA lending satisfactory to the community groups had been arranged. It is not difficult to imagine that the regulators did not want the severe criticism from Congress that would have followed their failure to assist community groups in reaching agreements with, and getting commitments from, banks that had applied for these approvals. In statements in connection with mergers it has approved, the Fed has said that commitments by the bank participants about future CRA lending have no influence on the approval process. A Fed official also told the Commission's staff that the Fed did not consider these commitments in connection with merger applications. The Commission did not attempt to verify this statement, but accepted it at face value from a Fed staff official. Nevertheless, there remains no explanation for why banks have been making these enormous commitments in connection with mergers but not otherwise.

The largest of the commitments, in terms of dollars, were made by four banks or their predecessors—Bank of America, JPMorgan Chase, Citibank, and Wells Fargo—in connection with mergers or acquisitions as shown in table 14.

Given the enormous size of the commitments reported by NCRC, the key questions are: (i) how many of these commitments were actually fulfilled by the banks that made them, (ii) where are these loans today, and (iii) how are these loans performing?

Currently, in light of the severely limited Commission investigation of this issue, there are only partial answers to these questions.

Were the Loans Actually Made?

The banks that made these commitments apparently came under pressure from community groups to fulfill them. In an interview by Brad Bondi of the Commission's staff, Josh Silver of the NCRC noted that community groups did follow up these commitments.

Bondi: Who follows up . . . to make sure that these banks honor their voluntary agreements or their unilateral commitments?

Silver: Actually part of some of these CRA agreements was meeting with the bank two or three times a year and actually going through, "Here's what you've promised. Here's what you've loaned." That would happen on a one-on-one basis with the banks and the community organizations.[91]

Nevertheless, when the Commission staff asked the four largest banks for data on whether the merger-related commitments were fulfilled and in what amount, most of the banks supplied only limited information. They contended that they did not have the information or that it was too difficult to get, and the information they supplied was sketchy at best.

90. http://www.community-wealth.org/_pdfs/articles-publications/cdfis/report-silver-brown.pdf.
91. Interview of Josh Silver of the National Community Reinvestment Coalition, June 16, 2010.

TABLE 14
ANNOUNCED CRA COMMITMENTS IN CONNECTION WITH A MERGER
OR ACQUISITION BY THE FOUR LARGEST BANKS AND THEIR PREDECESSORS

Final bank	Acquired or merged bank/entity with a corresponding announcement of a CRA commitment	CRA commitment (year announced and dollar amount)
Wells Fargo	First Union acquired by Wachovia	2001 ($35 b.)
	SouthTrust acquired by Wachovia	2004 ($75 b.)
JPMorgan Chase	Chemical merges with Manufacturers Hanover	1991 ($72.5 m.)
	NBD acquired by First Chicago	1995 ($2 b.)
	Home Savings acquired by Washington Mutual	1998 ($120 b.)
	Dime acquired by Washington Mutual	2001 ($375 b.)
	Bank One acquired by JPMorgan Chase	2004 ($800 b.)
Bank of America	Continental acquired by Bank of America	1994 ($1 b.)
	Bank of America (acquired by NationsBank, which kept the Bank of America name).	1998 ($350 b.)
	Bank of Boston acquired by Fleet	1999 ($14.6 b.)
	Fleet	2004 ($750 b.)
Citibank	Travelers	1998 ($115 b.)
	Cal Fed	1998 ($115 b.)
		2002 ($120 b.)

SOURCES: Compiled by Edward Pinto from the NCRC 2007 report CRA Commitments, found at http://www.community-wealth.org/_pdfs/articles-publications/cdfis/report-silver-brown.pdf, NCRC testimony regarding Bank of America's $1.5 trillion in CRA agreements and commitments in conjunction with its 2008 acquisition of Countrywide found at http://www.house.gov/apps/list/hearing/financialsvcs_dem/taylor_testimony_-_4.15.10.pdf.

In some cases, the information supplied to the Commission by the banks, in letters from their counsel, reflected fewer loans than they had claimed in press releases to have made in fulfillment of their commitments. The press release amounts were: JPMorgan Chase (including WaMu, $835 billion), Citi ($274 billion), and Bank of America ($229 billion)—totaling $1.3 trillion in CRA loans between 2001 and 2008—and had been presented to the Commission by Edward Pinto in the Triggers memo.[92] No Wells Fargo press releases could be found, but in response to questions from the Commission, Wells provided a great deal of data in spreadsheets that could not be interpreted or understood without further discussion with representatives of the bank. However, the Commission terminated the investigation of the merger-related CRA commitments in August 2010, before the necessary data could be gathered. For this reason, the Wells data could not be unpacked, interpreted in discussion with Wells officials, or analyzed.

---

92. Edward Pinto, exhibit 2 to the Triggers memo, dated April 21, 2010, http://www.aei.org/docLib/Pinto-Sizing-Total-Federal-Contributions.pdf.

After I protested the limited efforts of the Commission on this issue in October 2010, the Commission made a belated attempt to restart the investigation of the merger-related CRA commitments in November. However, only one bank had responded by the deadline for submission of this dissenting statement. As with the bank responses, additional work was required to understand the information received, and there was no time, and no Commission staff, to follow up.

As a result of the dilatory nature of the Commission's investigation, it was impossible to determine how many loans were actually made under their merger-related CRA commitments by the four banks and their predecessors. This, in turn, impeded any effort to find out where these loans are today and hence their delinquency rates. It appears that in many instances the Commission management constrained the staff in their investigation into CRA by limiting the number of document requests and interviews and by preventing the staff from following up with the institutions that failed to respond adequately to requests for data.

Where Are These Mortgages Today?

Where these loans are today must necessarily be a matter of speculation. Some of the banks told the FCIC staff that they do not distinguish between CRA loans and other loans, and so could not provide this information. Under the GSE Act, Fannie and Freddie had an affirmative obligation to help banks to meet their CRA obligations, and they undoubtedly served as a buyer for the loans made by the largest banks and their predecessors pursuant to the commitments. In a press release in 2003, for example, Fannie reported that it had acquired $394 billion in CRA loans, about $201 billion of which occurred in 2002.[93] This amounted to approximately 50 percent of Fannie's AH acquisitions for that year.

In the Triggers memo, based on his research, Pinto estimated that Fannie and Freddie purchased about 50 percent of all CRA loans over the period from 2001 to 2007 and that, of the balance, about 10–15 percent were insured by FHA, 10–15 percent were sold to Wall Street, and the rest remain on the books of the banks that originated the loans.[94] Many of these loans are likely unsaleable in the secondary market because they were made at rates that did not compensate for risk or lacked mortgage insurance—again, the competition for these loans among the GSEs, FHA, and the banks operating under CRA requirements inevitably raised their prices and thus underpriced their risk. To sell these loans, the banks holding them would have to take losses, which many are unwilling to do.

What Are the Delinquency Rates?

Under the Home Mortgage Disclosure Act (HMDA), banks are required to provide data to the Fed from which the delinquency rates on loans that have high interest rates can be

93. "Fannie Mae Passes Halfway Point in $2 Trillion American Dream Commitment; Leads Market in Bringing Housing Boom to Underserved Families, Communities," http://findarticles.com/p/articles/mi_m0EIN/is_2003_March_18/ai_98885990/pg_3/?tag=content;col1.

94. Triggers memo, p. 47.

calculated. It was assumed that these were the loans that might bear watching as potentially predatory. When Fannie and Freddie, FHA, Countrywide, and other subprime lenders and banks under CRA are all seeking the same loans—roughly speaking, loans to borrowers at or below the AMI—it is likely that these loans, when actually made, will bear concessionary interest rates, so that their rate spread would not be reportable under HMDA. It's just supply and demand. Accordingly, the banks that made CRA loans pursuant to their commitments have no obligation to record and report their delinquency rates, and, as noted above, several of the large banks that made major commitments recorded by the NCRC told FCIC staff that they don't keep records about the performance of CRA loans apart from other mortgages.

However, in the past few years, Bank of America has been reporting the performance of CRA loans in its annual report to the SEC on form 10-K. For example, the bank's 10-K for 2009 contained the following statement: "At December 31, 2009, our CRA portfolio comprised six percent of the total residential mortgage balances, but comprised 17 percent of nonperforming residential mortgage loans. This portfolio also comprised 20 percent of residential net charge-offs during 2009. While approximately 32 percent of our residential mortgage portfolio carries risk mitigation protection, only a small portion of our CRA portfolio is covered by this protection."[95] This could be an approximation for the delinquency rate on the merger-related CRA loans that the four banks made in fulfilling their commitments, but without definitive information on the number of loans made and the banks' current holdings, it is impossible to make this estimate with any confidence. In a letter from its counsel, another bank reported serious delinquency rates on the loans made pursuant to its merger-related commitments ranging from 5 percent to 50 percent, with the largest sample showing a 25 percent delinquency rate.

Further investigation of this issue is necessary, including investigation of the role of the bank regulators, in order to determine what effect, if any, the merger-related commitments to make CRA loans might have had on the number of NTMs in the U.S. financial system before the financial crisis.

---

95. Bank of America, 2009 10-K, p. 57.

PART IV

Conclusion

~

This dissenting statement argues that the U.S. government's housing policies were the major contributor to the financial crisis of 2008. These policies fostered the development of a massive housing bubble between 1997 and 2007 and the creation of 27 million subprime and Alt-A loans, many of which were ready to default as soon as the housing bubble began to deflate. The losses associated with these weak and high-risk loans caused either the real or apparent weakness of the major financial institutions around the world that held these mortgages—or PMBS backed by these mortgages—as investments or as sources of liquidity. Deregulation, lack of regulation, predatory lending, or the other factors that were cited in the report of the FCIC's majority were not determinative factors.

The policy implications of this conclusion are significant. If the crisis could have been prevented simply by eliminating or changing the government policies and programs that were primarily responsible for the financial crisis, then there was no need for the Dodd-Frank Wall Street Reform and Consumer Protection Act of 2010, adopted by Congress in July 2010 and often cited as one of the important achievements of the Obama administration and the 111th Congress.

The stringent regulation that the Dodd-Frank Act imposes on the U.S. economy will almost certainly have a major adverse effect on economic growth and job creation in the United States during the balance of this decade. If this was the price that had to be paid for preventing another financial crisis, then perhaps it's one that will have to be borne. But if it was not necessary to prevent another crisis—and it would not have been necessary if the crisis was caused by actions of the government itself—then the Dodd-Frank Act seriously overreached.

Finally, if the principal cause of the financial crisis was ultimately the government's involvement in the housing finance system, housing finance policy in the future should be adjusted accordingly.

Appendix 1

Hypothetical Losses in Two Scenarios
(No Feedback)

Scenario 1 is what was known to market professional during the second half of 2007. Scenario 2 is the actual condition of the mortgage market. Second mortgage/home equity loan losses are excluded.

Assumptions used:

Number of mortgages = 53 million;

Total value of first mortgages = $9.155 trillion;

Losses on Prime = 1.2% (assumes 3% foreclosure rate & 40% severity);

Losses on Subprime/Alt-A = 12% (assumes 30% foreclosure rate & 40% severity);

Average size of mortgage: $173,000

Losses in Scenario 1

Number of mortgages: 53 million
 Prime = 40 million
 Subprime/Alt-A = 13 million (7.7. PMBS million + FHA/VA = 5.2 million)

Aggregate Value:
 Prime = $6.9 trillion ($173,000 × 40 million);
 Subprime/Alt-A = $2.25 trillion ($173,000 × 13 million)

Losses on foreclosures: **$353 billion** ($6.9 trillion prime × 1.2% = $83 billion + $2.25 trillion subprime/Alt-A × 12% = $270 billion

Overall loss percentage: 3.5%

Losses in Scenario 2

Number of mortgages: 53 million
    Prime: 27 million
    Subprime/Alt-A:
        Original subprime/Alt-A: 13 million
        Other subprime/Alt-A: 13 million (10.5 F&F (excludes 1.25 million already counted in PMBS) + 2.5 million other loans not securitized (mostly held by the large banks))

Aggregate Value:
    Prime = $4.7 trillion ($173,000 × 27 million);
    Subprime/Alt-A = $4.5 trillion ($173,000 × 26 million)

Losses on foreclosures: **$596 billion** ($4.7 trillion × 1.2% = $56 billion + $4.5 trillion × 12% = $540 billion)

Overall loss percentage: 6.5%, for an increase of 86%

Note: No allowance for feedback effect—that is, fall in home prices as a result of larger number of foreclosures in Scenario 2. With feedback effect, losses would be even larger in Scenario 2 because a larger number of foreclosures would drive down housing prices further and faster. This feedback effect will likely cause total first mortgage losses to approach $1 trillion or 10 percent of outstanding first mortgages.

Appendix 2

Hypothetical Losses in Two Scenarios
(with Feedback)

Scenario 1 is what was known to market professionals during the second half of 2007. Scenario 2 is the actual condition of the mortgage market. Second mortgage/home equity loan losses are excluded.

Assumptions used:
Number of mortgages = 53 million;
Total value of first mortgages = $9.155 trillion;

Scenario 1:
    Losses on prime = 1.2% (assumes 3% foreclosure rate & 40% severity);
    Losses on self-denominated subprime & Alt-A = 14% (assumes 35% foreclosure rate & 40% severity);
    Losses on FHA/VA = 5.25% (assumes 15% foreclosure rate and 35% severity)

Scenario 2:
    Losses on prime = 1.6% (assumes 3.5% foreclosure rate and 45% severity);
    Losses on self-denominated subprime & Alt-A = 25% (assumes 45% foreclosure rate & 55% severity);
    Losses on FHA/VA & unknown subprime/Alt-A = 15% (assumes 30% foreclosure rate & 50% severity)

Average size of mortgage:
    Prime: $173,000 ($6.75 trillion/39 million)
    Subprime/Alt-A/FHA/VA: $182,000 ($2.4 trillion/13 million)

Losses in Scenario 1

Number of mortgages: 53 million
   Prime = 40 million
   Subprime/Alt-A = 7.7 million PMBS
   FHA, and VA = 5.2 million

Aggregate Value:
   Prime = $6.9 trillion ($173,000 × 39 million);
   Subprime/Alt-A = $1.7 trillion ($220,000 × 7.7 million)
   FHA/VA = $700 billion ($130,000 × 5.2 million)

Total expected foreclosures: 4.7 million (3% × 39 million + 35% × 7.7 million + 15% × 5.2 million)

Losses on foreclosures: **$360 billion** ($6.9 trillion prime × 1.2% = $83 billion + 1.7 trillion subprime/Alt-A × 14% = $240 billion + $700 billion × 5.25% = 37 billion)

Overall loss percentage: 3.9%

Losses in Scenario 2

Number of mortgages: 53 million
   Prime: 27 million
   Original subprime/Alt-A: 7.7 million
   FHA/VA: 5.2 million
   Other subprime/Alt-A: 13 million (10.5 F&F (excludes 1.25 million already counted in PMBS), 2.5 million other loans not securitized (mostly held by the large banks)

Aggregate Value:
   Prime = $4.7 trillion ($173,000 × 27 million);
   Original Subprime/Alt-A = $1.7 trillion ($220,000 × 7.7 million)
   FHA/VA = $700 billion ($130,000 × 5.2 million)
   Other subprime/Alt-A: $2 trillion ($154,000 × 13 million)

Total expected foreclosures: 8.4 million (3.5% × 27 million = 0.95 million, 45% × 7.7 million = 3.5 million, 30% × 13 million = 3.9 million)

Losses on foreclosures: **$890 billion** ($4.7 trillion × 1.6% = $60 billion + $1.7 trillion × 25% = $425 billion + $700 billion × 15% = $105 billion + $2 trillion × 15% = $300 billion)

Overall loss percentage: 9.8%, for an increase of 150%

About the Author

Peter J. Wallison is the Arthur F. Burns Fellow in Financial Policy Studies at AEI, and codirector of AEI's program on financial policy studies. He researches banking, insurance, and securities regulation. As general counsel of the U.S. Treasury Department, he had a significant role in the development of the Reagan administration's proposals for the deregulation of the financial services industry. He also served as White House counsel to President Ronald Reagan and is the author of *Ronald Reagan: The Power of Conviction and the Success of His Presidency* (Westview Press, 2002). His other books include *Better Parties, Better Government: A Realistic Program for Campaign Finance Reform* (AEI Press, 2009); *Competitive Equity: A Better Way to Organize Mutual Funds* (AEI Press, 2007); *Privatizing Fannie Mae, Freddie Mac, and the Federal Home Loan Banks* (AEI Press, 2004); *The GAAP Gap: Corporate Disclosure in the Internet Age* (AEI Press, 2000); and *Optional Federal Chartering and Regulation of Insurance Companies* (AEI Press, 2000). He also writes for AEI's *Financial Services Outlook* series.